SEA FIRE

THEY IMMEDIATELY ABANDONED THEIR
NETS AND BECAME HIS FOLLOWERS · MK 1·18

SEA FIRE

Tales of Jesus
and Fishing

Irene Martin

A Crossroad Carlisle Book
The Crossroad Publishing Company
New York

The Crossroad Publishing Company
481 Eighth Avenue, New York, NY 10001

Printed in the United States of America

The text is set in 11/15 Cheltenham. The display type is Triplex.

The woodcut facing the title page is by Helen Siegl. Used with permission.

Tater Tots is a registered trade mark.

Library of Congress Cataloging-in-Publication Data
Martin, Irene, 1946-
    Sea fire : tales of Jesus and fishing / Irene Martin.
        p.   cm.
    "A Crossroad Carlisle Book."
    Includes bibliographical references and index.
    ISBN 0-8245-2128-5 (alk. paper)
    1. Fishing – Religious aspects – Christianity. 2. Fishing – Biblical teaching.   I. Title.
BV4596.F5M28 2003
225.9′5 – dc21
                                                2003012313

1 2 3 4 5 6 7 8 9 10   10 09 08 07 06 05 04 03

Also by Irene Martin

Legacy and Testament
The Story of Columbia River Gillnetters
(Washington State University Press, 1994)

Beach of Heaven
A History of Wahkiakum County
(Washington State University Press, 1997)

Contents

And I saw the River over which every soul must pass
to reach the kingdom of Heaven,
and the name of that river was Suffering.
And I saw the boat which carries souls across that river,
and the name of that boat was Love.

—St. John of the Cross

Fishing with Jesus

The image of a slow-moving whirlpool occurs to me when I think of the fishing and other maritime portions of the New Testament. Such whirlpools commonly form where two or more bodies of water meet during the change of tides, or where geographical conditions force a current of water to reverse its course. The swirl and push and pull of the competing currents

The locus of the Gospels and their fishing stories is always Jesus.

causes a circular motion that transports debris, such as logs, marine vegetation, and even boats and entire nets, should they become caught in it. Like floating objects, the maritime stories and allusions in the New Testament are sometimes visible on the surface, disappearing in one Gospel and then resurfacing somewhat changed or seen from a different perspective in another. Sometimes an incident occurs only once and then sinks below the surface. A person may play a key role for a short time and then vanish forever from our sight. Some figures remain constantly visible close to the vortex, while others circle slowly on the distant periphery of the moving water. Yet there is always movement around a central point. The locus of the Gospels and their fishing stories is always Jesus.

Fishing is an occupation that tests limits. What seems like a test of physical limits, such as the need for sleep after many hours of fishing, the need for warmth, dry clothes, or relief from the pain of injury or the misery of seasickness, is actually a test of mental endurance. By the very nature of the occupation, tensions develop between the extremes of competition and cooperation, secrecy and openness, skill and luck, fear and the need to persevere. Fishing is an occupation founded on faith that the fish will be there, that we have the skill and knowledge to catch them, that a decent price will be forthcoming, and that we will not lose our lives in the process. And where faith is, somehow God must be there too.

The Fishing Occupation

> As he walked by the Sea of Galilee, he saw two brothers,
> Simon, who is called Peter, and Andrew his brother, casting
> a net into the sea — for they were fishermen. And he said
> to them, "Follow me...."   — Matt. 4:18–19

When the runs of salmon collapsed on the Columbia River in the 1990s, my husband and I chose to buy a boat and license and fish for salmon in Southeast Alaska in order to make a living. At the same time, I realized that I wanted to write a book about the biblical fishing community of which Jesus was a part. But after a year of research, my reaction was one of shock that so little attention had been paid to this part of Jesus' life.

We derive our knowledge of the Palestine of Jesus' time from a variety of sources, including the Bible, commentaries and scholarly works about the Bible, and various extra-canonical or apocryphal scriptures. The works of Josephus provide some historical background of the era. Archaeological exploration has produced new discoveries. Marine anthropology, with its body of findings about fishing folk throughout the world, offers valuable insights.

Yet as a fishing person myself, I knew that none of these gave the whole picture. I didn't want to know about just the temples and tombs of archaeology. I wanted to know about the crummy little restaurants and crummy little bars of the smelly little towns. I wanted to know whether fish were plentiful or whether fishing had fallen on hard times. Were fish prices low or high? I wanted to know whether women prepared the fish for market and whether they did the buying, selling, and trading. I wanted to know about the net racks, the smokehouses, and the fish gutting areas. With so little information available about the common life of first-century fishing towns, I had to resort to present-day fishing towns to find relevant examples. I had to supplement what was available with an imaginative reconstruction of the Gospel stories utilizing the fishing milieu I have worked in for thirty years. I spent long hours just sitting and observing, letting the gear and the water and the boats speak to me.

This technique is not as far-fetched as it might seem. Today's fisheries technologies mix the new with the ancient. On the Columbia River, for example, some people still use wooden floats and buoys, needles, and mesh boards, and in living memory some fish trap owners used stones to anchor the bottoms of nets.[1] Occasionally a fishing net will retrieve the wooden crosspieces of anchors made of stone from the early days when Columbia River sailing gillnet boats plied the river. These stone anchors, known as killicks, are still found in Newfoundland and elsewhere. Stone anchors with holes pecked in them found in the Sea of Galilee bear a remarkable resemblance to Native American stone anchors found in archaeological sites in the Pacific Northwest of the United States and Canada. Jesus' play on words about Peter's name, meaning a rock or stone, contains a possible reference to this vital part of a fishing boat's apparatus. A bronze hook found in an archaeological dig in Capernaum could replace one of today's stainless steel models. Wooden boats are still common in many of the world's fisheries, especially those that are artisanal and non-industrial.

I believe it is possible to study current fisheries technologies that employ ancient methodologies to better understand the biblical fishing culture.

The nets used today operate on the same principles as those in Jesus' time and earlier, although nylon updates the linen used in ancient times. The molding of lead into sinkers for the bottoms of nets or for weights in hook and line fishing hearkens back to the Bronze Age. The ancient lead sinkers[2] used on the

Sea of Galilee in the first century resemble those used on gear in twentieth-century North America. I once watched a cast net fisherman at work at the Place of Refuge on the island of Hawaii, using the same technique depicted on an Egyptian fresco from over thirty centuries ago. Government regulations required that sailboats be used in the salmon gillnet fishery of Bristol Bay, Alaska, until 1952. Sailboats are still extant in many of the world's fisheries.

The miracles on the water may still be miracles, even when viewed from the perspective of our time, but that perspective can never be identical to that of the first century.

Wood, stone, bronze, plastic: the technologies of the ages are employed in fishing, so that the past is always present. I believe it is possible to study current fisheries technologies that employ ancient methodologies, either in part or in whole, to better understand the biblical fishing culture. Present-day society has overlooked the contributions maritime cultures made in the biblical story, even though Jesus carried out much of his ministry in the fishing villages of Galilee with disciples who were fishermen. The Bible has contributed to our nautical language, as the stairs or ladder that pilots ascend when boarding a vessel is known as the "Jacob's ladder." The Bible's maritime influence has shaped non-nautical usage as well. For example, the main portion of a church is often referred to as the "nave" after the Latin term for ship. To make these and other discoveries, considerable detective work must occur.

Paradoxically, while current academic research neglects the fishing communities, customs, and practices of Jesus' time, the tourist industry has favored the locations where he traveled for pilgrimages for centuries. A well-known locale, the Church of the Multiplication at Tabgha, commemorates the story of the loaves and fishes. The Sea of Galilee and the Jordan River are common destinations. Our society is used to thinking about tourist stops and "the last great places," the Yellowstones and Grand Canyons. But I once heard an Eskimo fisherman sing a song in Inuktitut about "the little places." In their nomadic existence, the Inuit returned to the same places for brief periods of time in a seasonal round that focussed on obtaining food and other necessities. Fishermen of all cultures have their little places. An oddly shaped tree, a rock that is slightly different in color from those around it, a weathered piling that marks a particularly good area to anchor or to fish, all mark the little places that live in our memories. In Jesus' day, he and his disciples must have shared memories about the unnamed beaches, anchorages, and coves around the Sea of Galilee, the little places where they had breakfast, mended nets, sat and talked. Such places now bear the burden of two thousand years of romantic association and tourist promotion, so it is difficult to peel away the years back to when they were just little places that had meaning only for the surrounding fishing villages.

As I recall my memories of a fishing life, I realize that throughout the years there are echoes of Jesus' life experience. The shared meals, the rivalries, the competition and cooperation, the networks of friends and relatives, the ancient technologies, and the little places still exist in the fishing world. Searching for the universal experiences among the particular experiences of fishing, I ponder sleeping, eating, and traveling, all surrounded by water, which adds a different dimension to the ordinary. Natural phenomena on the water include water spouts, tide rips, whirlpools, sundogs, sudden storms, waves crashing on rocks, and phosphorescence, called sea fire by fishermen. I recall waking in the middle of the night to retie a line that was all silver sparkles from the phosphorus in the water. I played with the rope in the water for some time, swirling it around to make patterns. Marine phosphorescence is caused by blooms of marine plankton that give off minute flashes of light. Fishermen of two thousand years ago would not have known the scientific explanation for this saltwater phenomenon. The fact that I do does not diminish the wonder. However, it means that phenomena in the Bible may not have been perceived the same way then as they would be now, just as the little places may no longer be the same for us as they were for them. The miracles on the water may still be miracles, even when viewed from the perspective of our time, but that perspective can never be identical to that of the first century.

Despite some trepidation about reading too much into the past from a present-day viewpoint, I think exploration of the fishing life of the Bible is worthwhile. An old Columbia River gillnetter once told me, "You always fish your hunches."[3] Following that advice, I am going to follow my hunches as I go fishing for Jesus. Because I think he is to be found in fishing communities today just as he was two thousand years ago. I have been given a fishing life. I am hoping for a net full of God.

The Invisible Works of the Lord

They that go down to the sea in ships, that do
     business in great waters,
These see the works of the Lord, and his wonders in
     the deep.   — Ps. 107:23–24 KJV

After many years of research and reflection on the biblical fishing community of which Jesus became a part, I still react with surprise when I read the latest research on Jesus' life and find so little attention paid to that community. The plethora of scholarly work on peasant agrarian society during his time contrasts with the dearth of information regarding Mediterranean peasant fishing society. Countless works on the Eucharist focus on bread and wine but seldom mention fish, which was a major component of many of the Eucharist-like meals of the Bible. Perhaps only someone who has led a fishing life can understand a fishing life. After nearly thirty years of fishing on the Columbia River, Willapa Bay, Bristol Bay, and in Southeast Alaska, I have seen some of the maritime works of the Lord and his wonders in the deep.

Northrop Frye called the Bible "The Great Code."[1] I believe that within that code is another code, contained in the fishing portions of the Bible. Mysterious, elusive, this subcode is a story within a story, and the source for profound insight into Jesus' ministry. But our culture has lost a collective memory of something that was once very important, central even, in the lives of Jesus and his closest companions. The fish have become invisible.

What might a person of our era know about Jesus and the fishermen of the Sea of Galilee? Since most of us have not had the opportunity to travel in Israel or visit the area where Jesus lived and fished, our knowledge must necessarily be secondhand, from books, art, films, plays, music, and the poems and stories of others. The Bible obviously shapes our primary images. For me, *National Geographic* magazine contributed a great deal to my understanding of fishing on the Sea of Galilee in my pre-fishing days. My early *National Geographic* Jesus is a quaint individual who fished with outmoded technology, compared to modern times. When I researched later articles, the magazine presented progress in the region in the form of fish farms and the tourist trade. Supplanting the old-fashioned fishery images, more recent articles emphasize use of the Sea of Galilee as a source of water critical to Israel's well-being. Early articles in *National Geographic* focused on Israel and Galilee because of the Jesus connection, with fishing receiving minor attention. More recent articles spotlight Arab/Israeli relations, demonstrating that the Jesus connection has become much less important to an increasingly secular society.[2]

In the visual arts, three pictures formed my early images of fishing on the Sea of Galilee. The first, by Raphael, *The Miraculous Draught of Fishes,* shows five fishermen plus Jesus in two boats not much bigger than water skis. The fishermen are hulks with rippling muscles, and the boats resemble shallow skiffs, with the disciples standing on them as if they were platforms. A fine-featured Jesus lolls nonchalantly in the stern of one boat, despite the fact that it is sinking under the weight of fish. Since an ordinary man in the first century of the common era in Galilee probably stood about 166 cm. tall (approximately 5 feet, 4 inches), this picture contains little in the way of historic verisimilitude.[3] A far better picture, at least from a fishing viewpoint, is Rembrandt's *Christ in the Storm on the Sea of Galilee.* The boats are the correct size in comparison with the people in them, and they have room to work in. The third picture I love is Salvador Dali's painting *Saint John of the Cross.* Viewed from above, the audience, which includes Jesus on the cross, sees a boat with two fishermen and a net. I had never imagined the cross as a mast until I saw this painting. Other images that readers might have seen include the innumerable paintings and engravings that have appeared in illustrated Bibles over the years. The artists have frequently depicted Jesus as a somewhat effeminate person of refined features, compared with the coarse louts he is associated with. The boats vary in accuracy, with some resembling nothing ever sailed on any waters.

Church hymnody incorporates images that contribute to our stereotyping the fishing disciples as rustic bumpkins. A selection of examples includes "Jesus Calls Us," where St. Andrew leaves all for Jesus' sake; "They Cast Their Nets in Galilee" where fishermen are variously described as contented, peaceful, happy and simple; and "Dear Lord and Father of Mankind," which describes the "simple trust" of those who heard Jesus and rose up and followed him "without a word." Even in my pre-fishing days I was suspicious of the happy peasant connotations; after thirty years in the fishing community, I know how false this portrayal is.

The medium of film contributes to our inaccurate notions of Jesus and the disciples. Some films of biblical stories present a version of an ethereal Christ accompanied by tall, muscular, good-looking men who never sweat. Beautiful women provide a decorative backdrop. While I am being somewhat facetious here, I do believe that many of us have a stereotype of Jesus and his fishing disciples that has built up, layer by layer, from the cultural influences around us. I also believe that this stereotype of Jesus as movie star shields us from the reality of the fishing culture of Jesus' time and its influence on him.

Today's fishing culture in the United States is all but invisible, which contributes to our lack of understanding of Jesus' milieu. In a study by the Seamen's Church Institute of New York and New Jersey, the following paragraph describes the situation:

"There are probably less than 5,000 active merchant seafarers in the United States today. However, there are approximately 230,000 commercial fishers! These commercial fishers are, far-and-away, the largest segment of seafarers in the United States today. Yet, with a few notable exceptions, religious and other social service agencies ministering to seafarers here in the United States largely ignore commercial fishers.... The likely explanation [for this omission] is the natural inclination of such ministries to direct their efforts towards the "stranger amongst us" (the merchant seafarer) rather than towards the fisher/seafarer who is seen as a local with the same problems as other workers, e.g., a factory worker or farmer.

"But the truth is that the fisher/seafarer experiences many of the same problems that other seafarers face. They work at sea; they are often away from home for long periods of time; their work entails great danger; and, they are isolated from the rest of their community."[4]

Today's fishing culture in the United States is all but invisible, which contributes to our lack of understanding of Jesus' milieu.

Although the Seamen's study was completed in 1980, my experience indicates that it is not much out of date. Church and social service agency programs for fishermen are either nonexistent or hard to locate. Fishermen who arrive by boat in a strange town find few transportation services available to enable them to take part in the activities of the place. Fishing seasons on the west coast of the United States frequently open at noon on Sundays, so attending a church to make local connections is not possible. In my own denomination, the omission of the prayer for the burial of the dead at sea from the contemporary Book of Common Prayer speaks of a society largely unaware of the fishers in its midst.

Despite this neglect by others, however, fishermen frequently incorporate religious imagery into their occupation. Saints, such as St. Elmo, patron saint of sailors, figure prominently as boat names, along with phrases such as Blessed Assurance, Redeemer, Maranatha, Silver Chalice, Day Spring, Spirit, Faithful, Exodus, and Providence. Bumper stickers on fishermen's pickups sport phrases such as "Jesus was a gillnetter," "Jesus was a seiner," and "My boss is a Jewish carpenter." Crucifixes are common on vessels belonging to Catholic and Orthodox fishermen, and the old-fashioned blessing of the fleet still takes place in some harbors, although it is now more geared to tourists. Coastal churches may house models of fishing vessels, given in thanks for rescue from sea.[5] Many west coast U.S. fishermen I know still cling to the superstition of not beginning a sea voyage on a Friday, which is considered to be very bad luck. Even the atheists among them honor the ancient memory of the crucifixion on Good Friday.

Because of the demands of their craft, fishermen tend to socialize a great deal among themselves. Rafting together to cook and share a common meal is a familiar pattern. Fishermen frequently form radio groups to contact each other about fish locations, and will tend to travel together to a distant fishing ground both for safety's sake and for companionship. If a breakdown occurs, someone will probably know a nearby mechanic, someone else may know a carpenter, the local cannery's welder can make up a spare part, and other fishermen will help put a boat or net

24

together again so the vessel owner doesn't lose too much time on the water. These extended networks of contacts, relatives, friends of relatives, and families who may have moved from one fishing town to another, are all part of the web of life on the water.

Twenty centuries of cultural overburden have left us with stereotypes that do a disservice to our comprehension of the richness of the cultural background of Jesus' time. The fishing community he involved himself with was a vital component of his thinking, his life and his ministry. Trivializing his disciples by thinking of them as oafs ignores the special culture of which they were a part and which helped shape the events of the Gospels and the development of the early church. Fortunately, we now have the opportunity to trade our false images for a more realistic picture, by examining our stereotypes in the light of the knowledge provided by marine anthropology, archaeology, and history. We have new means for accessing the fishing disciples and the "wonders of the deep" that they experienced.

The Smell of Death and Money

While they were eating, Jesus took a loaf of bread, and after
blessing it he broke it, gave it to the disciples, and said,
"Take, eat; this is my body." Then he took a cup, and after
giving thanks he gave it to them, saying, "Drink from it, all
of you; for this is my blood of the covenant, which is poured
out for many for the forgiveness of sins."   — Matt. 26:26–28

One of the blocks to our understanding of the biblical
fishing story is the alienation of our predominantly urban society from primary sources of production. Rural
communities surrounded the Sea of Galilee of Jesus'
time. Fishing towns included Capernaum, Bethsaida,
Gadara, and Magdala. The last-named was the home
of Mary Magdalene. Its Hebrew name, Migdal Nunya,
means tower of fish. Its Greek name, Tarichaeae, means
salted fish or smoked fish. Imagine the ripe stench of
rotting fish guts, of sardines drying, of preservatives
used in boats, and of smoke from smokehouses. While
we would be appalled at such an odor today, such a
smell represented wealth in Jesus' time. Native Ameri-
cans named a certain beach on Washington's Olympic

peninsula the "stinkingest beach," but they meant it as a compliment, due to the large quantities of fish taken there. In the cannery towns of Alaska, British Columbia, and elsewhere, the familiar aroma of fish being processed is often referred to as the smell of money. I suspect the inhabitants of the Galilean fishing villages related similarly to their odoriferous surroundings.

One of the blocks to our understanding of the biblical fishing story is the alienation of our predominantly urban society from primary sources of production.

Some years ago I worked in a fisheries booth at the Oregon State Fair, where visitors expressed amazement at the display of fresh fish on ice. The universal urge on the part of the fairgoers to touch the brightly colored rockfish, salmon, and other species spoke to their lack of familiarity with food in its natural state. Our society has a sanitized view of killing and a separation from the knowledge that in order for us to eat, something else, plant or animal, must die. I have watched many salmon die in the fish locker at my feet, shivering in a last tremor before life fades. Beauty trembles into death. The fascination with death and violence on television and films, coupled with funeral customs that serve to separate us from any contact with the bodies of our loved ones, indicate a deep division in our souls about the confrontation with death.

A fishing culture, however, is intimate with death. On the night before he died, Jesus presented himself as food. His body was bread, his blood wine. For us to have food, to live, something must die. Jesus died. Raw primary production. Death was real to his fishing friends. They dealt with it every day and knew it when they saw it. A Columbia River fishermen put it well: "I still keep the first one [salmon]...There has to be a kind of spiritual relationship between the animal and yourself. Otherwise I think it'd drive you insane...because you really are killing and you have to have...an importance to what you're doing and say, 'Well, you're going to a good end. And nourishment and part of the cycle of continuing life.'"[1]

We fantasize about life that does not include death or suffering. Read *Glamour, Vogue,* and other magazines to discover how to erase all signs of aging. The American ideal of life, liberty, and the pursuit of happiness contains the germ of the notion that we can live without suffering. We create the illusion of life divorced from suffering in a variety of ways, including the way we think about food. Fruits and vegetables come to us from supermarkets, unblemished, produced on factory farms, with a long shelf life and in convenient forms not known in nature, such as Tater Tots. We consume food without flavor, buy fruit that

28

rots before it ripens, select avocados that feel like stones. What kind of metaphor for the Messiah is Wonder bread? Jesus asked, "What man, if his child ask for bread, will give him a stone, or fish, will give him a serpent?" His references are to the diverse and sometimes unwanted products of a fishnet: stones, fish, water serpents. Does Jesus as the lamb without blemish have any meaning for those who have never seen fruit, vegetables, meat, that are not perfect, for whom a blemish is an adolescent skin problem, readily treatable with innumerable products in the pharmacy?

What author Bob Pyle calls the "extinction of experience"[2] leads to a state of alienation from nature that in turn leads to today's ecological crises. The concept of "biophilia" ("the innately emotional affiliation of human beings to other living organisms")[3] insists that the natural world is necessary to human spiritual and emotional well-being. In Jesus' time, food production of one sort or another occupied large portions of the Jewish population who were involved with agriculture or fishing. Alienation from the natural world was not an issue for those who spent much of their lives working in it. Each year Jews celebrated the feast of Booths (Sukkot), when they went into the countryside and built temporary shelters of green leafy branches, reliving the wilderness experience of their ancestors during the Exodus. While the urban elite may have had less immediate contact with food production and the natural world than the mass of peasantry, there must still have been a strong link. Rituals at the Jerusalem temple, where the sacrifice of birds and animals occurred daily in God's honor, reinforced the connection between food and killing. God's butcher shop literally sanctified primary production.

Fishermen tend to measure death in terms of a catch of fish. The "Greenland Whaling Song" is a good example of this way of thinking:

And the boat capsized, and four men were drowned,
And we never got that whale, brave boys,
And we never got that whale. [Emphasis mine.][4]

The punch line emphasizes that the whalers missed the whale. Implied is the belief that the deaths would have been worthwhile if they had captured the whale. A nineteenth-century Columbia River saying corroborates this sense of values: "Salmon head is worth a dollar, man's head is worth nothing." Although spoken with a tone of bitterness, the saying recognizes that men were and are willing to risk their lives for fish, by fishing in storms, fishing in dangerously shallow areas, fishing in boats with faulty equipment, fishing on nothing more than a hunch that they are going to make a good catch. I have heard men laugh at themselves when the catch did not materialize. And sometimes a report comes in of someone who took a chance and did not live to laugh about it. Primary production.

30

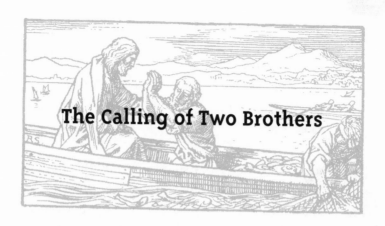

The Calling of Two Brothers

As he walked by the Sea of Galilee, he saw two brothers, Simon, who is called Peter, and Andrew his brother, casting a net into the sea — for they were fishermen. And he said to them, "Follow me, and I will make you fish for people." Immediately they left their nets and followed him.

— Matt. 4:18–20; see also Mark 1:16–18

The next day John again was standing with two of his disciples, and as he watched Jesus walk by, he exclaimed, "Look, here is the Lamb of God!" The two disciples heard him say this, and they followed Jesus. When Jesus turned and saw them following, he said to them, "What are you looking for?" They said to him, "Rabbi" (which translated means Teacher), "Where are you staying?" He said to them, "Come and see." They came and saw where he was staying, and they remained with him that day. It was about four o'clock in the afternoon. One of the two who heard John speak and

31

followed him was Andrew, Simon Peter's brother. He first found his brother Simon and said to him, "We have found the Messiah" (which is translated Anointed). He brought Simon to Jesus, who looked at him and said, "You are Simon son of John. You are to be called Cephas" (which is translated Peter).   — John 1:35–42

What are the dynamics of fishing communities that enabled Jesus to successfully recruit fishermen to his cause? In addition to the accounts related above, the Gospel of Luke (chapter 5, verses 1–11) has a story of Jesus' calling the disciples, a story that occurs when Jesus has just advised the fishermen to fish on the other side of the boat, and they succeed in hauling in a tremendous catch of fish. There are therefore three different stories of how Jesus chose his followers (Matthew and Mark's versions are identical).[1] Without some understanding of how fishing communities operate, none of the stories really seems very plausible. It strikes me as unlikely that Jesus would simply walk along the beach, see a strapping young stranger, invite him to come along, and be obeyed. Such a call has a mark of lunacy. Yet when we total the number of fishing disciples, there are as many as eight: Peter, Andrew, James, John, Philip, Nathanael/Bartholomew, Thomas the twin, and, as will be seen later, Matthew, the tax collector.[2]

One of the Gnostic documents, the Acts of Thomas, describes a Judas Thomas, asserted to be the twin of Jesus, as being a carpenter. The claims of Judas Thomas's identity need not concern us here, but the document's description of a carpenter's duties is illuminating: "In wood I can make ploughs and yokes and balances, goads and *ships and oars for ships, and masts and pulleys;* and in stone pillars and temples and royal palaces" (emphasis mine).[3]

Like farming, mining, logging, and other communities that cluster around an occupation, fishing communities develop values, customs, traditions, communication patterns, and other characteristics that differentiate them from other groups.

Notice how many of these items are maritime related. Jesus' occupation as a carpenter provided natural opportunities to associate with fishermen in order to provide them with the tools of their trade. Given that various passages of the Bible mention a variety of occupations current in Jesus' time, such as potter, farmer, vine-dresser, shepherd, innkeeper, weaver, merchant, soldier, scribe, priest, lawyer, and tentmaker, it seems strange that so many of his disciples came from one occupational group, i.e., fishermen, unless Jesus had some social or occupational connection with them.

To crack the biblical code, the field of marine anthropology offers insights into the occupational norms of fishing communities. Like farming, mining, logging, and other communities that cluster around an occupation, fishing communities develop values, customs, traditions, communication patterns, and other characteristics that differentiate them from other groups. Some common ethnographic characteristics of fishing cultures observed by marine anthropologists include the following:

1. Boats are "closed social systems," i.e., small areas that mandate the close involvement of the people aboard.

2. Crews are often kinship based, in order to reduce the stress of living in close quarters with others and to provide a more stable working team, as well as concentrating economic benefits within a family.

3. Mobility and isolation are dual factors in a fishing life. Boats travel from port to port and men are absent from home for extended periods of time.

4. Independence of thought combined with the need to cooperate in order to prosecute the fishing

operation are two characteristics common among fishermen. Frequently the need arises to make rapid decisions.

5. Fishing is a highly competitive operation, with fishermen being intensely egalitarian.

6. Fishing is a high risk occupation, with death and injury an ever-present reality.

7. Fishermen may feel isolated and separated from non-maritime people; in turn those who are land-based may consider fisher folk and fishing based communities as inferior.[4]

Applying this list of features to the fishing community of the New Testament illumines the calling of the fishing disciples. Jesus recruited his disciples the way a fisherman/entrepreneur would have recruited a crew. Andrew was a follower of John the Baptist, one of Jesus' relatives, who had himself baptized Jesus. When Andrew becomes part of Jesus' crew, Jesus calls Simon, Andrew's brother, and their two fishing partners, James and John. He also selects Philip, who was from the same city as Simon and Andrew. Philip in turn pulls in Nathanael, who was from Cana, where Jesus' first miracle occurred the following day at a wedding where they were all present.

The pattern of crew recruitment among relatives and their close associates would not be at all unusual for a contemporary fishing community. Until recently, we made up our crews from among my husband's relatives. Many U.S. fishermen still follow this custom, although it is becoming less common. However, it is still a behavior pattern in fisheries worldwide. The fishermen knew Jesus, either firsthand in their encounters with him (possibly through his occupation as carpenter) or through their encounters with his cousin, John the Baptist, or secondhand through gossip networks with their fishing kin. The genealogies of Jesus in the Gospels of Matthew and Luke attest that kin and relationships featured prominently in the society of his time.

Fishermen's mobility would have been a distinct asset to any itinerant prophet or teacher. Fishermen were accustomed to traveling and knew different areas of Galilee through their markets and suppliers of goods. Their families were used to isolation, as the men were frequently absent from homes and communities during fishing periods. Fishermen also spent a lot of time together on the waterfront while maintaining and repairing gear and boats. News spread from one community to the next by word of mouth from fishermen passing through the area, thus extending communication beyond the local region. Fishboats provided a quick getaway, in case things became uncomfortably tense in one territory. Herod Antipas's lands were only a boat ride away from

Philip's holdings. When Jesus cast out the demons named "Legion" in Gadara, a possible allusion to casting out Roman legions, a dangerous and subversive action, the nervous locals quickly invited him to leave. He then crossed to the other side of the lake (Mark 5:17–21). The crisscrossing of the lake occurs in a number of Gospel passages, placing Jesus in territories ruled by different authorities and allowing him to evade arrest. Access to boats was a significant advantage in ensuring his survival.

Fishermen's mobility would have been a distinct asset to any itinerant prophet or teacher.

Peter and Andrew owned a boat, and Zebedee, James, and John owned a boat. The two groups were in partnership, so they had to cooperate yet also be able to make quick and independent decisions. They worked together under the stress of close quarters and frequent physical danger and financial risk, but they were able to get along and hold their partnership together. As boat owners and entrepreneurs, they were accustomed to thinking both for themselves and for the partnership, particularly when using gear such as the seine and gillnet that require multiple people to operate. They may have pooled their catches in order to divide both profit and loss and to reduce risk. They exhibit many characteristics that would make them excellent "crew" for Jesus in his ministry: teamwork, risk taking, focus on a common goal, the ability to adjust to long absences from home, and their egalitarian ethic.[5] Peter seems to have been the natural leader of the group.

Why did the fishermen follow Jesus? Jesus' teachings would have had obvious appeal to their egalitarian nature. The incident involving the half-shekel tax to the Temple in Jerusalem (Matt. 17:24–27) illustrates this theme: "When they reached Capernaum, the collectors of the temple tax came to Peter and said, 'Does your teacher not pay the temple tax?' He said, 'Yes, he does.' And when he came home, Jesus spoke of it first, asking, 'What do you think, Simon? From whom do kings of the earth take toll or tribute? From their children or from others?' When Peter said, 'From others,' Jesus said to him, 'Then the children are free. However, so that we do not give offense to them, go to the sea and cast a hook; take the first fish that comes up; and when you open its mouth, you will find a coin; take that and give it to them for you and me.' "

Jews had to observe two systems of taxation, one to the Romans and one to the Temple. This story concerns the Temple tax. It parallels the story in Matthew 22:15–22, in which Pharisees ask Jesus whether it is lawful to pay tribute to Caesar. He asks one of his questioners to provide him with a coin, which has an image of Caesar on it, a transgression of the Jewish commandment to make no graven images. His comment was, "Give therefore to the emperor the things that are the emperor's, and to God the things that are God's" (Matt. 22:21).

The two stories regarding taxation complement each other, dealing with both the Roman and Jewish systems. The fish story in particular has strong egalitarian overtones, in that hook-and-line fishing was the one method of fishing available to all Jews, regardless of tribe. In the original division of Israel, the tribe of Naphtali gained exclusive fishing rights, except for this method.[6] Further, in this story the money is ritually clean, being a Jewish coin, a shekel, and coming from the sea. Our understanding as to whether a miracle occurred depends upon whether we believe God placed a coin in the fish's mouth, whether the coin was there because the particular fish was a bottom feeder and picked it up accidentally, or whether the value of the fish when sold equated to the temple tax. The underlying movement of the story, however, has less to do with fish and more to do with a subversive message regarding payment of the Temple tax. As *Harper's Bible Commentary* says: "The point of the story lies in the pronouncement. Roman citizens were exempt from taxation; taxes were paid only by the subject peoples. The disciples are citizens of the kingdom of

39

God and therefore (in principle) free from taxation. But to avoid scandal...they should voluntarily comply. They should not flaunt their freedom; to pay the tax does not involve any sacrifice of principle."[7]

It is easy to see why one who dealt so ably with both the Roman occupation, fishermen's egalitarianism, and the hated subject of taxation could be viewed as a potential military ruler, king, or Messiah. In addition, Jesus chose to relate to his followers through their occupation, by fishing with them. Jesus traveled in their boats to their communities, stayed in their houses, ate with them, and socialized with them. My guess is that he repaired their boats when necessary, made up an extra hand when needed on a fishing trip, and helped with the myriad tasks necessary to carry on the fishery. Fishing communities tend to be subcultures within a dominant culture. They are suspicious of outsiders. Only by taking part in their daily routines could Jesus have gained the trust and confidence of those fishermen whom he then recruited as his disciples.

The Sons of Thunder

James and John, the sons of Zebedee, came forward to him and said to him, "Teacher, we want you to do for us whatever we ask of you." And he said to them, "What is it you want me to do for you?" And they said to him, "Grant us to sit, one at your right hand and one at your left, in your glory." But Jesus said to them, "You do not know what you are asking. Are you able to drink the cup that I drink, or be baptized with the baptism that I am baptized with?" They replied, "We are able." Then Jesus said to them, "The cup that I drink you will drink; and with the baptism with which I am baptized, you will be baptized; but to sit at my right hand or at my left is not mine to grant, but it is for those for whom it has been prepared." When the ten heard this, they began to be angry with James and John. So Jesus called them and said to them, "You know that among the Gentiles those whom they recognize as their rulers lord it over them, and their great ones are tyrants over them. But

> it is not so among you; but whoever wishes to become great among you must be your servant, and whoever wishes to be first among you must be slave of all.   — Mark 10:35–44

Fishing has a great deal to do with playing for position and with traditional relationships. Because of fish movement patterns, being in the right spot at the right time can be critical to a good haul. As Bill Gunderson stated: "My grandfather passes on to my father and my father passes on to me, you don't lay out before 4 hours and 5 minutes, and you don't lay out after 3 hours and 50 minutes, because at precisely 4 hours and 50 minutes the fish will drop off of the sands and into the deep hole where your net is. And it's all timing, it was all timing within 5 minutes. And the fish haven't changed their pattern just because we have different boats and different gear and the sands have modified a little bit maybe.... But the fish still follow the same prehistoric or earlier habits of when they move off the sand into the channel and down."[1]

Similarly, Mendel Nun discusses fish migration patterns on the Sea of Galilee that dictate where fishermen fish during certain seasons and the type of gear they use.[2] The enormous accumulation of local knowledge stored up over the generations and passed on orally through families and kinship lines cannot be emphasized enough. The fishermen who are best at remembering this knowledge and utilizing it effectively by making decisions based on constantly changing conditions are the ones who obtain consistently high catches. "He has a mind like a filing cabinet," is a phrase applied to such highliners.

Not only does one have to be aware of where the fish are, one has to be aware of where the other fishermen are. Fishermen observe each other and develop an interior monologue that goes something like this: "That's the fourth day in a row that I've seen Bob over on the west side of the bay in that cove. He must be getting fish there or he wouldn't keep going back. Maybe I'll head over there tomorrow and see what's going on." The radio groups and spotter planes in Bristol Bay represent the acme of this type of fishing. Fishermen literally hire airplane pilots to spy on other fishermen. The pilot then radios the captain to tell him who is catching fish and at what location. The captain then decides whether it is worth it to travel to another location and vie for a lucrative fishing spot with those already there.

What James and John were doing in squabbling over who will sit at Jesus' left and right hand in his kingdom was a form of playing for position, a preemptive strike over Peter and Andrew and the other disciples. Even more fascinating is the version in Matthew 20:20–27, when Zebedee's wife, the mother of James and John, asks for this same favor. Whether there were one or more incidents of jockeying for this prestigious post we cannot know. However, a fishing family openly competing for an advantageous position is entirely consonant with fishermen's behavior, even though it may bring down on them the ire of the rest of the community for being overtly aggressive. What Jesus tells them in fishing terms is that everyone in his kingdom is in the same boat, and if they want to be great, they must be servants, just like the hired crewmen of Zebedee.

The issue of who was to be great in the kingdom, however, never really left the disciples during Jesus' lifetime. On the very night before he died, we read that a quarrel broke out among them as to who was to be greatest (Luke 22:24). To illustrate the different reality he envisioned, Jesus washed their feet, the job of a slave. Competition among fishermen is frequent in fishing circles, but a captain who takes the place of the lowliest crew member is quite unlikely. "Fiddler's Green," a song about a fisherman's idea of heaven, contains the line "You lie at your leisure, there's no work to do, and the Captain's below making tea for the crew."[3] Not an everyday occurrence. Jesus attempted to break through his followers' traditional norms by the sheer shock value inherent in washing their feet, the last thing they would have expected from a leader. Many of Jesus' actions are congruent with what we know to be the norms of fishing communities. However, the reverse is also the case; he was willing to violate those norms to make a point.

One phrase used to refer to James and John is their nickname, the "Sons of Thunder." Most interpretations dwell on their supposed rowdiness, loud voices, and noisiness.[4] This is entirely possible, I suppose, but I am more inclined to think of it as a nickname that refers to their occupation. The fishermen I know frequently give their companions nicknames to indicate some facet of their fishing expertise or personality. Some fishermen excel in fishing in bad weather, times when other fishermen prefer to stay at home or on the anchor. Under the right circumstances, fish may be moving during a storm, and it may be possible to make a good haul then. I suggest thinking of James and John as being willing to fish during bad weather, including during a thunderstorm; this is at least as plausible an interpretation of this passage as their supposed vocal volume. Being known as sons of thunder might indicate their skill at fishing in dirty weather.

The Three Who Followed

The next day Jesus decided to go to Galilee. He found Philip and said to him, "Follow me." Now Philip was from Bethsaida, the city of Andrew and Peter. Philip found Nathanael and said to him, "We have found him about whom Moses in the law and also the prophets wrote, Jesus son of Joseph from Nazareth." Nathanael said to him, "Can anything good come out of Nazareth?" Philip said to him, "Come and see." When Jesus saw Nathanael coming toward him, he said of him, "Here is truly an Israelite in whom there is no deceit!" Nathanael asked him, "Where did you get to know me?" Jesus answered, "I saw you under the fig tree before Philip called you." Nathanael replied, "Rabbi, you are the Son of God! You are the King of Israel!" Jesus answered, "Do you believe because I told you that I saw you under the fig tree? You will see greater things than these."

— John 1:43–50

Philip came from the port town of Bethsaida; Nathanael, also frequently identified as Bartholomew, came from Cana. Nathanael is listed in the Genealogies of the Twelve Apostles as being of the house of Naphtali,[1]

46

known for fishing connections. Philip and Nathanael/Bartholomew are usually mentioned together in scripture. Nathanael appears in John's Gospel in the final breakfast on the beach. Philip may have been one of the unnamed companions in this episode. Tradition usually associates the two with the fishing occupation. Thomas, also known as Didymus, the Twin, is associated either with fishing or with carpentry.[2] The latter occupation in turn was closely allied with fishing, in the days when boats were made of wood. We know few details of these disciples' lives from scripture, but the pattern of crew recruitment outlined in scripture suggests to me that Philip and Nathanael/Bartholomew followed fishing as an occupation. Thomas's fishing and carpentry connections help him fit into the maritime world of Galilee. We know him today by the nickname of "Doubting Thomas."

The one detail we do have about the calling of Nathanael concerns a fig tree. Jesus saw him "under the fig tree." This bit of trivia is one of those maddening, inexplicable details that has niggled at me for years. Why on earth would Jesus mention seeing Nathanael under the fig tree? What fig tree? Why a fig tree? Where was the fig tree? Of all the people in Israel who were sitting under fig trees at any given moment, why would he notice Nathanael? The one clue I have found occurs in *The Rob Roy on the Jordan,* by John MacGregor. In his travels in his canoe on the Sea of Galilee, MacGregor came across a waterfall that emptied into the Sea of Galilee, at a place called Ain et Tin, the Fount of the Fig-tree, as it was shaded by an old fig tree.[3] His journey took place in the mid-nineteenth century. It is a great leap to assume that this particular place was the fig tree mentioned in scripture, but MacGregor does say that there were a number of springs and waterfalls with trees nearby that emptied into the lake. Is this one of the little places that was familiar to fishermen? Perhaps accessible only by boat, it may have been a well-known fishing locale. I know of such places in Alaska and elsewhere, where a waterfall may attract fish, due to higher oxygen levels in the turbulent water. Trees hide fish from predators, and the insects that drop from them make good fish food. Fishermen often give favored fishing spots and anchorages colloquial names, such as Black Rock, the Gold Mine, the Diamond, the Stump Drift, or the Notch. Was the Fig Tree one of those names?

We are too far removed from the customs of Jesus' time to do anything more than speculate about the passage of the fig tree and its meaning. I am uncomfortable with speculation, as it extends the imagination past what I think is a reasonable boundary. Yet in my mind's eye, I see Nathanael in a small boat near a waterfall, casting a net under an old fig tree, unaware that he is being watched by Jesus.

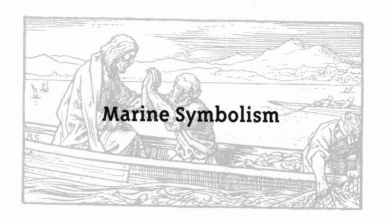

Marine Symbolism

For just as Jonah was three days and three nights in the belly of the sea monster, so for three days and three nights the Son of Man will be in the heart of the earth.

— Matt. 12:40

Jesus uses the ancient story of Jonah to link the past and the future of his listeners, likening Jonah's sojourn for three days in the whale's belly to his own death and three day interment. In his employment of literary allusion, he is the forerunner of the numerous commentators and authors who have dealt with the watery imagery in the Bible, especially in its association with death.

Scholarly and artistic treatments of biblical marine symbolism range from Fraser's *The Golden Bough* to T. S. Eliot's poem, "The Wasteland." Fish play a relatively minor role in most of these works. Northrop

Frye mentions fish in connection with the great deluge: "The question of what happened to the fish in the Deluge is an old puzzle: in one aspect of symbolism, the flood has never receded and we are all fish in a symbolically submarine world of illusion.... [In baptism] the one being baptized is symbolically drowned in the old world and awakens to a new world on the opposite shore. Similarly, there is a dimension of the symbolism in which the redeemed, after the apocalypse, are able to live in the water of life, as they now live in the air."[1] In this passage, human beings are likened to fish in water and fish out of water, making a connection between fish, water, and Baptism. This connection is an ancient one. Early Christians used the fish as a symbol for Christ, based on a Greek cryptogram, *Iesous Christos Theou Yios Soter* (Jesus Christ, Son of God, Savior) or I.Ch.Th.Y.S., the Greek word for fish. Tertullian wrote: "But we are little fishes, called after our great fish Jesus Christ. We are born in water and can only survive by staying in water."[2]

The "great fish" referred to here is written as Ichthus or Ichthys.[3] The fish symbol appeared in catacombs and elsewhere to identify followers of the faith. It survives today as a car ornament. Its twin, adorned with little legs, indicates a Darwinian owner.

Other uses of nautical symbolism include both the fish and the anchor. Early Christians viewed the anchor as a symbol for the cross. Both fish and a dove adorn it on early seals and in the catacombs. The fish was also a symbol of the Eucharist. Curiously, the radiance of light surrounding Jesus in early paintings, the *vesica,* refers to a fish bladder. To Christians, the image of a ship symbolized the church. The mast and yardarm represented the cross, and occasionally St. Peter appears at the helm.[4] In the Episcopal Diocese of Olympia in western Washington, where I reside, the official seal bears a ship, while the Anglican Diocese of Caledonia in British Columbia features salmon on its seal.

The fish symbol appeared in catacombs and elsewhere to identify followers of the faith.

Symbols of some of the saints provide piscatorial icons to reflect on. Pictures of St. Andrew may show him with two fish in his hands. The device for Simon (not Simon Peter) is a fish on a book, depicting him as a person who successfully fished for converts to the Gospel. The symbol for St. James is the scallop shell. The scallop moves by clapping its two halves together. It appears in numerous classical paintings with Venus riding on one of its halves. All other bivalves such as clams, oysters, and mussels are sedentary in their adult stage. The scallop is the only bivalve that travels in water, and became a symbol of travel, missionary journeys, and baptism.

The psychologist Carl Jung devoted a large portion of his book *Aion* to arcane fish symbolism in scripture and in astrology. Jung mentions that the early church thought of believers as being fish, with Jesus as the great fish. The baptismal font was known as the *piscina,* or fish pond. Today we use this term to refer to a sink in a church that drains into the ground, where leftover communion elements such as water and wine are poured. Jung also describes Jesus as the first fish born in the new age of Pisces and the last lamb to die as the era of Aries, the ram, was coming to a close.[5]

Jung also points out that Jesus' name is the equivalent of Joshua. In the Old Testament Joshua ben Nun meant Joshua son of the fish, so Jesus' very name is an allusion to his predecessor. Both Christian monks and disciples of Jewish rabbis were known as fish. Jung even discusses Jesus as the bait on God's hook, the cross.[6] He produces a mass of source material and commentary that indicates that the fish was a powerful symbol in the Jewish, Christian, and pagan world for centuries. His insight that, in astrological terms, Jesus ushered in the age of Pisces, helps us better understand the culture of the pagan world of the first millennium, in which fisheries played a more prominent role than they do today.

Unfortunately, illuminating symbolism can delve into the arcane to the point where credulity is strained. An example is Edmund Leach's treatment of James and John, the sons of Zebedee, also known as Boanerges, the sons of thunder. By a series of torturous connections, he posits that many of the early Greek-speaking readers of the Gospel of Mark would have associated the two with the Greek and Roman twin gods (Gemini). He concludes that James and John did not actually exist but are literary devices designed to create echoes of Old Testament mythology and meld with Greco-Roman religious thought.[7]

While I find such associations fascinating and a help in appreciating the literary qualities of the Bible, I approach them cautiously. There is a danger of drowning in literary allusions and missing the story itself. The fishing incidents with James and John convince me of their existence. What I really want to know is what was going on in the first-century fishing community of Galilee that attracted Jesus and in turn attracted followers to him.

The Fish of Galilee

One of his disciples, Andrew, Simon Peter's brother, said to him, "There is a boy here who has five barley loaves and two fish. But what are they among so many people?" Jesus said, "Make the people sit down."...Then Jesus took the loaves, and when he had given thanks, he distributed them to those who were seated; so also the fish, as much as they wanted.
— John 6:8–11

Western society's lack of knowledge about basic fishing technologies leads to one of the difficulties in writing about the fisheries of the New Testament, which is the lack of precision in many translations. In English, the word "net" appears as the common rubric for any kind of net, such as a seine or a cast net, but the two are not the same in Greek. Similarly, the word "fish" appears as both *ichthus* and *opsarion* in the New Testament, the former being fresh and the latter preserved fish, providing shades of meaning that elude the reader of an English translation.

I cannot claim that the fishing story of the New Testament follows any logical progression, as the writers of the Gospels exhibit varying degrees of familiarity with the subject and in any case were not writing a technical manual on how to make a good haul on the Sea of Galilee. But they were aware of the fishing culture of their time, as demonstrated in their use of correct terminology for different kinds of net. Further, considerable detail appears in the Book of Acts in the New Testament regarding marine travel, storms on the Mediterranean, safe anchorages, and water depths, indicating the importance of the marine world in early Christianity.[1] However, even the Gospel writers employed common terms such as "fish" to describe a multiplicity of species that inhabited the Sea of Galilee.

Fishermen today use terms for fish in much more specific ways, though they are generally geared to the dominant species in their region. For example, in Newfoundland, the term "fish" means cod; all other species receive their proper name. On the west coast of the United States, the term "salmon" has multiple meanings. It may be a generic term for the five species of salmonids found along the coast, or it may specify chinook, the largest and generally most valuable of the five species, with the others being called by their proper names, such as coho, chum, pinks, or sockeye. There exist also a myriad of colloquial names for salmon, such as kings, silvers, dogs, humpies, reds, and blueback. Native American names such as *tyee* or *keta* salmon are also used. While I would expect that such richness of vocabulary existed on the Sea of Galilee, the Gospel writers confined themselves to generic terms.

Considerable detail appears in the Book of Acts in the New Testament regarding marine travel, storms on the Mediterranean, safe anchorages, and water depths, indicating the importance of the marine world in early Christianity.

The Sea of Galilee is actually a freshwater lake. Several kinds of fish that were commercially important in the lake during Jesus' time were the musht (tilapia), barbels, and sardines. Musht migrate in the cooler winter months toward the northern part of the lake, where various hot springs keep the water at a higher temperature. In particular, they inhabit the area near Capernaum known as the springs of Tabgha, which were under Herod Antipas's jurisdiction in Jesus' time. These fish move in schools. Today they are also known as St. Peter's fish. Three types of barbels, members of the carp family, also lived in the lake. Sardines, the third commercially important species, were salted or pickled to preserve them. Magdala, under the control of Herod Antipas, was the center of this processing industry.[2]

Catfish also grew in the lake, but because they have no scales, they were not kosher and could not be eaten by Jews.[3] Kosher fish had to have fins and scales. Shellfish are classed as non-kosher and are therefore forbidden.[4] However, there is no reason to suppose that catfish or other non-kosher products did not supply the substantial gentile populace in the area. Fresh fish went to the local market. Preserved fish were consumed locally and also were exported. They were a major source of protein in the region and throughout the Roman empire.

Fish populations and their abundance or scarcity, catch makeup, and markets are the building blocks of any fishery. The Bible's authors provide no specific information regarding any of these. But these three key components dominated the daily lives of Jesus' fishing disciples.

Three Herods

In the fifteenth year of the reign of Emperor Tiberius, when Pontius Pilate was governor of Judea, and Herod was ruler of Galilee, and his brother Philip ruler of the region of Ituraea and Trachonitis, and Lysanias ruler of Abilene, during the high priesthood of Annas and Caiaphas, the word of God came to John son of Zechariah in the wilderness.

—Luke 3:1–2

The brokers for change, to fit Galilee into the Roman mold, were the three Herods. In 47 B.C.E. the Romans appointed Herod the Great as governor of Galilee. The Romans had held Palestine as a province for some time and had divided it into several smaller provinces. Herod was an Idumean Jew, that is, a descendant of citizens of the small state of Idumea who had been forced to convert to Judaism after their defeat by the Hasmonean king, John Hyrcanus. During his career, Herod the Great consolidated his holdings, which included Galilee and Judea. His massive building programs included construction of the port city of Caesarea Maritima, which required immense engineering skills, and the fortress and palace at Masada.[1] He commenced the rebuilding of the Temple in Jerusalem. All of these projects required enormous amounts of labor and materials. He was able to keep peace and order in the land, although not in his own family, as he killed one of his wives and three of his sons. As the Roman Emperor Augustus observed, "It is better to be Herod's pig than his son." Herod the Great died in 4 B.C.E., succeeded by his three remaining sons, Archelaus, Philip, and Herod Antipas. His territory was once again divided: Archelaus became Ethnarch of Judea, Philip controlled part of northern Palestine, and Herod Antipas became Tetrarch of Galilee and Perea.

Herod Antipas shared his father's passion for architecture. Among his projects was the rebuilding of Sepphoris, a town only four miles from Nazareth, where Jesus grew up. Sepphoris had been destroyed during a revolt after the death of Herod the Great. Several scholars have pointed out the possibility, even probability, that Jesus and his father Joseph, both builders, may have been involved in the work at Sepphoris, and it can hardly have been unknown to them. Sepphoris contained thirty thousand inhabitants, including Jews, Arabs, Greeks, and Romans and was a powerful seat of government for the Herodian family.[2] The Bible mentions Joanna, wife of Herod's steward Chuza, as one of Jesus' strong supporters, after Jesus healed her of demon possession. Jesus himself refers to Herod as "that old fox." Did Jesus meet Joanna and Chuza in connection with the Sepphoris project? Herod Antipas built Tiberias as his capital city on the west shore of the Sea of Galilee. He was the ruler who put Jesus' kinsman, John the Baptizer, to death, due to unsavory internal family politics concerning the wife of Herod's brother Philip.

The third Herod was Herod Agrippa, brought up in the Roman court, who became Tetrarch of northern Palestine in 37 C.E. and also eventually ruled Judea and Samaria, thus regaining all the territory once ruled by his grandfather, Herod the Great.[3] While the boundaries of their possessions continually shifted, depending upon who was in favor with the rulers in Rome and who was not, all three Herods supported and prosecuted the trend toward the increased urbanization of Palestine. Their policies put pressure on the people and resources of the area for nearly a century.

The architectural splendors built during the lengthy rule of the three Herods contrast with the murkiness of their public affairs. Issues of taxation, religious freedom, famines, and outbreaks of revolts arose throughout the decades they were in power and were met with typical brutality by the ruling classes. Gamaliel mentions an uprising led by Judas of Galilee and Theudas (Acts 5:37). Josephus provides us with details of one such revolt, known as the First Jewish Revolt, in Galilee between the years of 67–70 C.E. The leader, Jesus, son of Sapphias, led "a seditious tumult of mariners and poor people."[4] It seems safe to assume that they were the people most heavily oppressed by the Roman occupation, as they had been a few decades earlier in the time of Jesus, the son of Mary. The Bible refers to day laborers in the market place whom no one would hire. The fishing servants who accompanied Zebedee suggest that some workers no longer had access to the means of production but were forced to work for someone else who did.

The First Jewish Revolt culminated in a battle at Tarichaeae, commonly called the Battle of Migdal. Through plot and counterplot the Jewish fighters whittled away at the Roman army and prepared their fishing boats to engage in a battle on water. Ultimately, however, they lost the battle, and the fleet was sunk. Survivors were tricked into giving themselves up and were either killed or sold as slaves.[5]

The reign of the Herods pushed the fisheries within their control into economic chaos. The result was the impoverishment of the marine communities of Galilee, and the creation of a population that was desperate enough to revolt against the Roman empire.

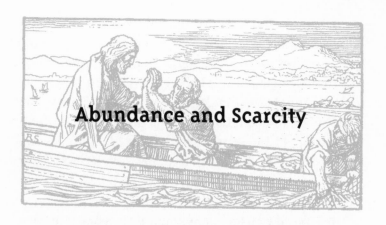

Abundance and Scarcity

Once while Jesus was standing beside the lake of Gennesaret, and the crowd was pressing in on him to hear the word of God, he saw two boats there at the shore of the lake; the fishermen had gone out of them and were washing their nets. He got into one of the boats, the one belonging to Simon, and asked him to put out a little way from the shore. Then he sat down and taught the crowds from the boat. When he had finished speaking, he said to Simon, "Put out into the deep water and let down your nets for a catch." Simon answered, "Master, we have worked all night long but have caught nothing. Yet if you say so, I will let down the nets." When they had done this, they caught so many fish that their nets were beginning to break. So they signaled their partners in the other boat to come and help them. And they came and filled both boats, so that they began to sink. But when Simon Peter saw it, he fell down at Jesus' knees, saying, "Go away from me, Lord, for I am a sinful man!" For he and all who were with him were amazed at the catch of fish that they had taken; and so also were James and John, sons of Zebedee, who were partners with Simon. Then Jesus said to Simon, "Do not be afraid; from now on you will be catching people." When they had brought their boats to shore, they left everything and followed him.

— Luke 5:1–11

The Sea of Galilee (also known as the Lake of Tiberias, Kinnereth, Lake Gennesareth, Lake Ginnosar, and many other variants) formed a natural boundary between Galilee, inhabited by both Gentiles and Jews, and the largely gentile territories of Gaulanitis and the Decapolis.[1] A historian named Flavius Josephus, writing in the first century C.E., described the lake as follows: "Now this lake of Gennesareth is so called from the country adjoining it. Its breadth is forty furlongs and its length one hundred and forty; its waters are sweet and very agreeable for drinking.... There are several kinds of fish in it, different both to the taste and the sight from those elsewhere; it is divided into two parts by the river Jordan.... The country also that lies over against this lake hath the same name of Gennesareth; its nature is wonderful as well as its beauty; its soil is so fruitful that all sorts of trees can grow upon it.... One may call this place the ambition of nature."[2]

The ambition of nature! In this phrase, Josephus invokes images of fruitfulness, plenty, and beauty and also subliminally introduces the concept of the exploitation of natural resources. With a foot in both the Jewish and Roman worlds, he sums up the clash of world views between the two cultures. The Jewish understanding of creation was central to their monotheistic belief: God created, God saw that creation was good and blessed it, and God rested. Jews believed that fish were created on the fifth day and received the first blessing, animals and humans were created on the sixth day and received the second blessing, and the Sabbath was created on the seventh day, and was also blessed. Fish, humans and animals, and the Sabbath were thus linked in threefold blessing.[3] The Romans, by contrast, focused on agrarian production and extensive trade networks to feed a colossal empire, aided and abetted by a pantheon of gods, some of whose actions were downright unsavory in Jewish eyes. The theologies of the two cultures vis-à-vis the natural world could not have been more different.

The Romans' relentless urbanization of Galilee changed Jewish peasant agrarian and fishing life. The life of the small village was coming into contact and conflict with larger urban areas. Society for the Jewish people appeared fragmented. As Howard Kee points out: "The Temple and its priestly establishment had become a colossal commercial enterprise, with its hierarchy maintaining control through cooperation with the Roman imperial authorities. The Essenes had retreated in despair to the Judean desert to maintain their purity as the faithful remnant of God's people, while awaiting God's intervention and their own vindication. The Pharisees had shifted the focus of their religious life from the Temple cult to the family and voluntary gatherings in homes or public halls (synagogues). Clearly, there was a series of competing schemes to bring divine order out of the chaos of Jewish life under Roman rule, and to do so in a way that would confirm God's control of the history of the covenant people and of the created order."[4]

The Romans' relentless urbanization of Galilee changed Jewish peasant agrarian and fishing life.

John Crossan states, "Roman urbanization dislocated the traditional peasant way of life and pushed individuals from poverty into destitution, from small landowner into tenant farmer, from tenant farmer into day-laborer, and from day-laborer into beggar or bandit."[5] The Herodian building achievements in the two cities of Sepphoris and Tiberias, "built within about twenty years and twenty miles of each other,"[6] dramatically affected the surrounding area. Jonathan Reed notes, "In terms of food alone, the agricultural practices of Galilee were completely realigned and stretched with the foundation of these two cities. The picture of numerous self-sufficient farms or hamlets in Galilee radically changed. The entire agricultural focus turned to feeding Sepphoris and Tiberias."[7] Curiously, no scholar has focused on what urbanization did to the peasant fishing community.

A common observation is that fishermen who are adept at a multiplicity of gear types are responding to fish populations that are fluctuating or on the decline.

I believe that the ecological changes brought about by the Herodian building programs and their accompanying population increases had a profound effect on the fisheries of the Sea of Galilee. While the cost in money and labor for these massive construction projects must have been enormous, even more insidious would have been the pressure on natural resources, especially wood in a wood-poor region, to provide building materials. Both cultivation and forest clearing depleted vegetation in Galilee as noted by Arav for the period of 3000 B.C.E. to 500 C.E.[8] By 100 C.E. wood was so scarce in the Roman Empire that cremation was forbidden.[9] Archaeological evidence from an analysis of the construction of the Galilee boat, which utilized salvaged and inferior woods for repair work, indicates a typical fisherman's and boat carpenter's adaptation when faced with a shortage of good timber or a need to economize.[10]

Capernaum was built in the first century B.C.E., Tiberias in 18 C.E. Philip the Tetrarch elevated Bethsaida to his capital city "at least in part as a fishing establishment to rival the already established Galilean fishing center in Tarichaeae, which was both a city and a center of a toparchy that included Capernaum."[11] All of these projects point to a population explosion around the lake and an increased demand, and hence competition, for fish. Such population explosions invariably bring the concomitant problems of sewage disposal and water usage. Tiberias in particular must have posed a problem. It boasted a population of between thirty thousand and forty thousand people. It was situated on the western shore of the Sea of Galilee, adjacent to the migration route for musht, a commercially important fish. These fish migrate during colder weather to areas where warm water, rising from thermal underwater springs, increases the temperature sufficiently to sustain them. One such area is the springs at Tabgha, near Capernaum. Musht also migrate to avoid areas of the lake that contain little oxygen during certain times of the year, especially July.[12] While environmental changes in this area remain undocumented for the first century, alterations must have occurred around the lakeshore due to runoff caused by removing vegetation to accommodate new buildings and cutting trees for construction materials. Increased sewage effluent created by the burgeoning population would undoubtedly have drained into the lake. Such changes would have adversely affected water quality, fish stock abundance, and fish migration patterns.

While it is not possible to state here with absolute certainty what natural phenomena were occurring on the Sea of Galilee at the time of Jesus,[13] it should be noted that documentation for other periods of time indicates the presence of earthquakes, tsunamis, changing water levels, and a changing shoreline on the lake.[14] Landslides in the canyon along which the Jordan River flows periodically choked the gorge, temporarily impounded the river and caused sudden catastrophic floods when the water broke through, depositing debris and building a delta.[15] Climatic variations that increased or decreased annual rainfall also affected the lake. Due to its location near a number of geological faults, the area was dynamic, not static. The lake's coastline was subject to rapid change.[16] All of these phenomena would have affected water quality, water quantity, and the population dynamics of the lake's fish. A constantly changing natural environment coupled with manmade changes occurring during the intense building programs of the region must have had a destabilizing influence both on fish populations and the communities that depended upon them.

I also infer that fish stock were collapsing in the lake by examining the fishermen's behavior, particularly in their use of multiple types of gear. The Bible describes four types of gear in use: the seine, the gillnet, the cast net, and hook-and-line. The main point here is that the disciples were familiar with a variety of fishing techniques, strategies, and gear types. A common observation is that fishermen who are adept at a multiplicity of gear types are responding to fish populations that are fluctuating or on the decline. In order to make a living, fishermen have to learn how to use more than one kind of gear, so that they adapt when one species or another proves to be scarce.[17] When salmon prove scarce in British Columbia or Southeast Alaska, for example, fishermen may gear up for crab or shrimp pot fishing, or go hook and line fishing for halibut if they have a quota. On the Columbia River, if biologists predict a poorer than average salmon run, some fishermen may decide to fish sturgeon instead, or they may concentrate on smelt in the winter months.

The multiplicity of gear mentioned in the New Testament hints at an ecological trauma wherein fish were scarce and fishermen had to use every possible means to make a living. Investing in several kinds of gear would have increased their costs, possibly putting them at the mercy of moneylenders. Not every fisherman is equally adept at each gear type, so a fisherman who was not particularly skilled in more than one kind of fishing gear would have been rapidly marginalized economically in a situation of a declining resource. Such a person might have sought work as a crew member for another fisherman, or work mending or hanging gear or doing a bit of boat carpentry. Due to the scarcity of raw materials, the increased cost of maintaining a wooden boat would also adversely impact profits. It appears to me that the evidence suggests a period of scarcity rather than abundance on the Sea of Galilee, a period of economic marginalization for all but the top producers. Why else would the disciples have been astonished at a large catch of fish, as stated in Luke's Gospel?

I believe that the ecological changes brought about by the Herodian building programs and their accompanying population increases had a profound effect on the fisheries of the Sea of Galilee.

By fast forwarding to the present, we can see what happens to fish when human populations impinge on their habitat. The Columbia River is a prime example of a once enormously productive river, where salmon runs by the millions returned annually. With the buildup of cities and industries that polluted the waters, the damming of the river and its tributaries for irrigation, flood control, and hydroelectric power, and the siltation of spawning beds due to mining and timber operations, today's runs are a fraction of their former abundance. Management agencies have reduced or eliminated fishing seasons in a vain attempt to halt the decline, with limited success as habitat issues are the heart of the problem. In comparison, Canada's Fraser River, which has no mainstem dams and little irrigation, is a striking contrast, as the Fraser's salmon runs have remained healthy. When I compare the Columbia River with some of the wild Alaska rivers, I am overcome with a sense of what an abundance of fish was once here in the Columbia, and what has been lost, not just in terms of fish but also in terms of community life.

I remember the first time we went up the Wrangell Narrows in Southeast Alaska in our fishing vessel, the *Blue Mist*. Salmon were leaping everywhere. We could not avoid seeing them except by closing our eyes. I knew then that it was a mistake to think that there was only one Eden. The God who created such abundance is a God of unimagined splendor, the God of Eden everywhere. In the Bible it appears that abundance, not scarcity, is a sign of God's manifestation. Manna, flocks of quail, and water gushing from a rock announce God's presence in the Exodus. Many baskets of leftovers remain after feeding the five thousand.

The millions of mussels we crunched over to view the petroglyphs on the beach near Petersburg, the acres of huckleberries near St. John, the richness of the seafood we caught daily, the Northern lights, and sea fire, all attest to this God. The northern voyage to Alaska shows us annually what abundance is, and it shocks us into the knowledge that it was once like that on the Columbia. And I suspect it was something very like a collapse of fish stocks and with it a collapse of the small communities' way of life that occurred on the Sea of Galilee.

The Herods of biblical times set in motion the urbanization of Galilee, which in turn changed land use patterns, and, by extension, community patterns of use of the fisheries resources on the Sea of Galilee that were part of age-old custom. Their alteration of the Galilean habitat produced ecological changes in the lake that significantly reduced its fish productivity. All segments of the fishing society were affected profoundly. Galilee, which Josephus called "the ambition of nature," contained the lake where the fishermen were saying, "We fished all night and caught nothing." The words I hear are filled with pain.

The Roman Impact
on the Fishing Business

Now Philip was from Bethsaida, the city of Andrew and
Peter.   — John 1:44

He went down to Capernaum, a city in Galilee, and was
teaching them on the sabbath.... After leaving the syn-
agogue he entered Simon's house.   — Luke 4:31–38

Individual decisions are embedded in history's mo-
ments. The fishing disciples had the misfortune to
live in a time of chaos on the Sea of Galilee due to
the Roman occupation of their country. To understand their plight as control of the fisheries of the
lake changed, imagine yourself listening to the following dialogue in Bethsaida, the original home of Simon
Peter and Andrew.

Simon: "I just heard the news. It's official. Philip is in
charge of this part of the country now. He's planning
on making Bethsaida the center of his fishing industry,
and we're restricted to his part of the lake."

Andrew: "What in Gehenna are we going to do?
There's no way the limited fishing grounds here can
support us all."

Simon: "The only thing I can think of is to see if we can form a partnership with Zebedee and his boys over in Capernaum. Maybe that way we'd still be able to fish at Tabgha. And we can try to get Mary over in Magdala to salt the sardines for us."

Andrew: "And how many people do we have to bribe to do it? How do you figure we'll be able to pay the taxes? We'll have to pay Philip his share here in Bethsaida, then give a share to that vulture tax gatherer Matthew in Capernaum. He'll want his cut before the money gets passed on to Herod Antipas. Fish are scarce; it's not like we're making a bundle as it is. And with Archelaus in charge of Judea, we're going to get taxed again if we try to take fish there to sell at the Temple."

Simon: "But we'd have a better market at Capernaum. With the garrison full of Roman soldiers, we could sell our fish there, and since they're gentiles, we could get rid of the unclean fish and make a profit doing it. And we'd have access to the market in Tiberias, too."

Andrew: "That profit's going to get eaten up bribing those same soldiers to look the other way when we cross the boundaries into Herod's territory. The profit margin isn't there. I think we should just relocate to Capernaum."

Simon: "Easy for you to say. I've got a wife and her widowed mother to look after. What a mess. Damn Romans sure don't understand the fishing business."

The Romans indeed did not understand the fishing business. The Roman Empire was an agrarian Empire, with a heavy reliance on the importation of foodstuffs to feed the population in the city of Rome itself. Galilee exported vegetables, grain, olive oil, and salted fish, particularly from Magdala. In turn Galilee imported grain from Egypt, beer from Babylon, and wines and purple dye and other items from Tyre on the nearby Mediterranean coast.[1] The free flow of commerce was of utmost importance to the smooth functioning of the Empire. However, the Palestine of Jesus' time was deeply divided along racial, ethnic, linguistic, and religious lines. Zealots, Sadducees, Greeks, Pharisees, Samaritans, Idumean Jews, and followers of charismatic religious leaders such as John the Baptizer, form a colorful procession through the pages of the Bible. Galilee itself was divided into upper and lower Galilee, with most of Jesus' ministry being carried out in lower Galilee, one of the most densely populated areas of the Roman Empire.[2]

The fishing communities around the Sea of Galilee that are mentioned in the Gospels are Capernaum, Bethsaida, Magdala, and Gergesa or Gadara. Fishing communities, to quote Carolyn Creed, "are occupational communities. In occupational communities social relations of production largely determine the sociocultural framework of everyday life and therefore the social context in which individuals act."[3] Our

North American emphasis upon individual freedom makes it difficult for us to comprehend the importance that community held for the fishing disciples and the tension they felt with the rapid community change brought about by the Roman occupation.

Our North American emphasis upon individual freedom makes it difficult for us to comprehend the importance that community held for the fishing disciples and the tension they felt with the rapid community change brought about by the Roman occupation.

Because the borders of the Sea of Galilee fell within two different political jurisdictions after the death of Herod the Great, a new system of regulations must have affected fishing on the lake. Philip attempted to develop the fisheries of Bethsaida during his reign[4] in competition with his brother Herod Antipas who controlled Capernaum and Magdala. While no details regarding how this division affected fishing regulations exist, the Bible notes that Peter and Andrew and possibly Philip the disciple left Bethsaida and settled in Capernaum. Did Herod Antipas actively recruit fishermen to his territory? Did they leave Bethsaida in order to regain access to the rich Tabgha fishing ground? Was the regulatory climate or taxation system more favorable there than in Philip's territory? Clearly, larger markets were there, as the population increases near the lake occurred predominantly in the areas under Herod's control.

W. H. Wuellner mentions two ways of marketing fish. "Royal fishermen" delivered specific amounts of fish at certain times to a royal household or to a temple, including the one at Jerusalem. Zebedee is said to have had a market at the Jerusalem temple.[5] "Tax fishing" was the other method, wherein fishermen had a contract with a tax collector and had to pay a tax on each catch, but could then trade in the local market for their own profit.[6]

With the division of territory after the death of Herod the Great, conflict must have arisen over marketing fish, as Jerusalem was now in another political jurisdiction, Judea. The confusion among fishermen around the lake can only be imagined. Now they were confronted by three different rulers instead of one, each of whom controlled access to different markets. Two of these rulers controlled access to fishing grounds and were actively competing with each other. The fishermen had religious obligations to provide fish to the Jerusalem Temple, which competed with the opportunity to profit in an expanding local market (which probably included significant numbers of gentiles).

All these conditions must have caused tremendous tension in the fishing industry.

If we suppose that legend is accurate and Zebedee had a market at the Jerusalem Temple, what kind of pressure were his sons under when they left him to follow Jesus, whose Temple relations were not always amicable? What kind of pressure did this put on Peter and Andrew, their partners, in choosing where to market their fish? These questions have no definitive answer, but they illustrate the fundamental societal disturbances that Roman rule must have brought to the fishing communities.

Additionally, it seems plain to me that the fishing communities paid a tremendous emotional toll as their way of life collapsed. A survey done of fishermen after the collapse of the Columbia River fisheries in the late twentieth century can serve as a surrogate to appreciate the emotional strain of Roman control and reorganization of the Galilee fisheries. Fishermen responded to a question concerning the impact of the change on the Columbia River in the following ways:

"It has been a very sorrowful time for our family. It's like having a death in the family."

"We still eat, but we've wiped out our savings and our debts mount.... We'll probably lose our house before it's over."

"The few individuals left with the mental stamina to try to protect the industry, are doing so at enormous cost to themselves, both financially and psychologically."

"Had to move, sell home, start totally over."

"Have had to deal with depression in my life because of lost fishing opportunities and added financial burden."[7]

A survey done of fishermen after the collapse of the Columbia River fisheries in the late twentieth century can serve as a surrogate to appreciate the emotional strain of Roman control and reorganization of the Galilee fisheries.

I recall visiting a little Alaskan community several years ago when my husband and I had a few days off and decided to go exploring. It had a beautiful anchorage, but the village was starting to acquire the scruffy look of a place where not much is happening. The bustle and energy that accompany a thriving economic base were missing. Poor fish prices for the previous several years had begun to take their effect, coupled with regulatory changes that destabilized markets. That evening the rain began. A heron on a boom log nearby hunched his shoulders against the falling drops until an unwary seagull tried to perch near him. The grouchy heron chased him off, clearly not wanting company on such a miserable evening. The fog rose in solid masses from the various clefts among the trees. The rain made slow dreary indentations in the water. I don't think I was ever in a place that felt more isolated and hopeless.

Is this what Peter and his friends saw happening to their beloved little communities in Galilee? Were they faced with the choice of staying in their home community and starving, or leaving and starting all over? Did they consider phasing out of fishing? Did the move to another community mean they had to leave their extended families and networks of friends behind, and compete with the fishermen already established in a new locale? The Bible is silent about their anguish and dismay over their plight. However, of the accounts left to us, it is astonishing to realize how many times the fishing industry or maritime trades were at the root of the problems the Romans had to deal with in Galilee.

More Herods

When his daughter Herodias came in and danced, she pleased Herod and his guests; and the king said to the girl, "Ask me for whatever you wish, and I will give it." ...Immediately she rushed back to the king and requested, "I want you to give me at once the head of John the Baptist on a platter." ...Immediately the king sent a soldier of the guard with orders to bring John's head.   — Mark 6:21–27

I saw some modern-day Herods once and felt the impact of a lifestyle totally alien to my own. Tied near our fishing vessel, the *Blue Mist,* in Wrangell Harbor one morning was an enormous yacht hailing from a notorious Latin American tax haven for the very wealthy. On the afterdeck, three middle-aged men were eating breakfast with three young and beautiful women. A uniformed crew of at least six were washing windows, serving breakfast, carrying luggage up the gangway, and generally doing the things servants do. No one responded as my husband and I passed and said hello. Despite the ostentation, this one did not qualify as the biggest yacht we had seen, as it lacked a helicopter deck and accompanying helicopter. All the crew members were attractive young men and women. Was this the contrast Jesus saw in his time, between the poor and destitute and the Herods with every luxury, young beautiful women as commodities, servants to take care of everything, and no attachment to the landscape or its people?

Kent amplified my thoughts that day with his own perspective. "The one thing money cannot buy is youth. However, it can buy young people to surround oneself with so that one can live in an illusion of youthfulness." Ponce de Leon spent years searching for the fountain of youth in Florida. Our modern-day Herods have surrounded themselves with young people, who mirror back youth to them. Was Herod the Great's killing of his own children and the slaughter of the innocents an attempt to prevent the realization of his own aging process? The Herods in the floating palace near us reminded me that the desire for luxury and the aphrodisiac of youth is not confined to Jesus' era.

Fishing Gear

As he walked by the Sea of Galilee, he saw two brothers, Simon, who is called Peter, and Andrew his brother, casting a net into the sea—for they were fishermen.

—Matt. 4:18; see also Mark 1:16

He saw two boats there at the shore of the lake; the fishermen had gone out of them and were washing their nets.

—Luke 5:2

The Bible describes four types of gear in use on the Sea of Galilee in Jesus' time. I characterize them as encircling gear (the seine, or *sagene*), entangling gear (trammel and gillnet, *diktyon, diktya*), entrapment gear (cast net, *amphlibestron*) and hook-and-line, or enticement gear. I have fished trammel nets, gillnets and hook-and-line, and have observed the use of seine and cast nets in various locations, including Hawaii, British Columbia and Alaska. Mendel Nun, an authority on

83

the fisheries of the Sea of Galilee, provides details on the use of each of these types of gear in New Testament times. Some of these uses continue today, and all of them have been used within living memory. As Rousseau and Arav point out: "Fishing methods did not change much from biblical times until shortly after World War II. What was observed in the late 1940s could be traced back to Egypt of the 3rd millennium B.C.E."[1]

Georgia Maki, a woman net mender on the Columbia River, corroborated this statement from the perspective of a fishery hundreds of years and thousands of miles removed from Galilee: "When I was about nineteen or twenty, I had net mending all the way from Astoria to Corbett. At that time, fishermen used linen to make nets, but because it is a natural fiber, the linen would eventually rot. Fishermen now use nylon nets, most of which are made in Japan. But the main idea of a net, that four strands make a mesh, is still the same as it was hundreds of years ago. The fishnet has changed little in design over the years. Many people don't realize that the commercial fishing industry is a very old trade."[2]

The seine, sometimes called a dragnet, requires a boat, usually about 8.5 meters by 2.5 meters, and is fished in the daytime. The choice of location as to where to lay out the net is crucial, as a smooth bottom surface is essential in order to avoid snagging and tearing the net. The boat sets out from shore paying out a rope to which the net is attached. At the end of the rope, the boat turns and lays out the seine parallel with the shore. Then the boat returns to shore, paying out another rope attached to the opposite end of the seine. Each end of the net is hauled in to shore by part of the crew. The fish that the net has encircled are trapped and dragged to shore, where fishermen sort them and divide them into shares, each person getting one or more shares according to his investment and responsibility in the enterprise.[3] After fishing, fishermen commonly spread their seines out to dry on the shore.[4]

The trammel net is a type of gillnet, where three layers of web are held together by a corkline for flotation along the upper edge and a leadline which causes the lower edge of the net to sink so the net is held perpendicular in the water. Fish swim through the larger outer mesh and strike the backwall of finer smaller mesh. The slack backwall forms a bag between the larger meshes so the fish is caught. The net is composed of several units or shackles of gear of uniform size attached to each other. Such nets work best at night, when the fish cannot see the web. The following day, the trammel net is taken to shore and washed free of silt and hung up to dry and mended if necessary. It was the only kind of net that was washed. Set gillnets, using one wall of web, in which fish are caught by their gills, were also used.[5]

In employing a cast net, the fisherman throws a circular net over the water, an operation requiring considerable practice. Due to the weight of the leads attached to its bottom edge, the net opens out into an umbrella-like shape and sinks, trapping fish between the wall of web and the bottom of the lake. The fisherman may dive down and retrieve the fish by hand by pulling them through the mesh, or may gather up the net by the weighted bottom and bring it into the boat or ashore and remove the fish.[6] This kind of net is ubiquitous worldwide and its origins are of great antiquity, being found among native inhabitants of the Northwest Coast, native Hawaiians, and in Europe, Asia, and ancient Egypt.[7]

Only one instance of hook-and-line fishing appears in the New Testament. Hook-and-line fishing may involve bait or may consist of moving the hook up and down in the water ("jigging") so that the fish is snagged by the moving hook. Not enough detail is given in the biblical account to tell which method was used and what kind of fish was caught.[8]

The salient point crucial to understanding fishing gear is to recognize that each method of gear relies on fish habits and patterns of behavior for success. A gillnet relies on a fish putting its head into the mesh, attempting to escape by backing out, and then getting caught by its gills or back fin. Hook and line fisheries depend on a fish striking a lure or bait without stopping to examine whether it really is food or whether there is a hook attached. Fish tend to bite first and ask questions later, a survival technique that serves them well when food is scarce, as the quickest fish gets the most to eat. Not all fish will bite on a lure, nor will the fish that are attracted to lures necessarily bite in all seasons. The seine relies on a fish habit of trying to escape a net by diving to the bottom, rather than swimming around the end of the net. Since the seine fishes from top to bottom, there is no escape for the fish under the net. Night fishing with a gillnet takes advantage of fish's limited night vision. Each gear type is adapted to known fish behavior characteristics. It is not too much of a stretch to recognize that fishing for men could follow the same format, analyzing people's behavior characteristics and developing methods for their "capture," and gathering them into the kingdom of God.

One final note: The Greek term for mending a net found in Matthew 4:21 and Mark 1:19 has the same root as the word "perfecting" or "equipping" the saints found in Ephesians 4:12, "restore" in Galatians 6:1, and associations with preparing and repairing.[9] The connection between fishing and discipleship is more evident in the Greek than the English, a lost echo of a distant time.

Jesus the Fisherman

When he had finished speaking, he said to Simon, "Put out into the deep water and let down your nets for a catch." Simon answered, "Master, we have worked all night long but have caught nothing. Yet if you say so, I will let down the nets." When they had done this, they caught so many fish that their nets were beginning to break. So they signaled their partners in the other boat to come and help them. And they came and filled both boats, so that they began to sink. But when Simon Peter saw it, he fell down at Jesus' knees, saying, "Go away from me, Lord, for I am a sinful man!" For he and all who were with him were amazed at the catch of fish that they had taken; and so also were James and John, sons of Zebedee, who were partners with Simon. Then Jesus said to Simon, "Do not be afraid; from now on you will be catching people." When they had brought their boats to shore, they left everything and followed him.

— Luke 5:4–11

Can we use present day fishing experiences akin to those in the Bible to think about the texts that pertain to fishing? I think it is possible, provided they are not offered as a definitive interpretation, but as a fresh way of thinking, an experiment, just as one might choose to fish a slightly different piece of gear in a certain spot on the hunch that there might be fish there. For example, the story of the large draught of fishes has meaning for me because it parallels experiences of my own fishing life. However, although the rubrics in the chapter heading of the Gospel usually list this event as a miracle, I find it hard to accept that interpretation.

The miracle here is not the large catch, nor the type of gear used. It is the personal story of Peter.

As a fishing person, what grips me about this story is not the large numbers of fish that are caught, but Peter's response to Jesus' advice to lay out a gillnet, normally fished at night, in the daytime. "Master, we have worked all night long but have caught nothing. Yet if you say so..." (Luke 5:5). What is the tone here? What does Peter's voice sound like? Respectful obedience? Somehow I doubt it. Instead, I hear Peter using sarcasm. He was undoubtedly tired from a night's work, frustrated and angry at himself for having missed the fish, and arrogant about his expertise. He may also have been frightened about a decline in the fisheries and anxious about the future.

The inner dialogue I hear going on in Peter's mind, and probably those of the other fishermen at Jesus' suggestion goes like this: "We're the fishermen. We're the ones who toiled all night using all our skill and good gear and caught nothing, and now an upstart rabbi from nowhere is trying to tell us where to look and what to do. And telling us to use a trammel net, rather than a seine, in broad daylight yet. Well, I'll just show him. I'll prove to him there's nothing there. We'll just let those nets down and show him a thing or two. It's not as easy as it looks. He needs to realize that he may know scripture, but we know what's what on Kinneret."

Reading further into the text, the qualities of patience and perseverance are evident in the fact that Peter can say truthfully, "We have worked all night long but have caught nothing" (Luke 5:5). Patience is a virtue when waiting for fish to be in the right place, or waiting for just the right combination of wind and tide in order to set the net out just right. Fishermen know that given certain weather and water conditions, fish will be in a certain place at a certain time. They carry enormous amounts of local data in their memories. In the fishermen's eyes, Jesus was a novice; being able to fill the nets would have had an enormous impact upon them. He proved himself to them on their terms.

And Peter is wrong. And he admits it. "Go away from me, Lord, for I am a sinful man!" (Luke 5:8). For me as a fishing person, this is the pivotal moment in the scene. It takes courage and humility for the captain of a vessel to admit in front of his crew that he was wrong. To confess it as a sin of pride opens him up to the possibility of redemptive grace. Jesus' use of the trammel net, when the seine would have been the more common net to use in daylight, is one of those technical breakthroughs that occurs occasionally in fisheries. I think of the introduction of the otter trawl for smelt fishing on the Columbia River, but there are numerous examples of gear deployment in unusual situations that have made fishing history. The miracle here is not the large catch, nor the type of gear used. It is the personal story of Peter.

Jesus in turn can be viewed as thinking like a fisherman in determining the shape of his ministry.

Let me use an example from my own fishing experience. Some years ago, my husband and I were fishing at the mouth of the Columbia River. The fishing fleet caught huge numbers of salmon that night, and after we had delivered our fish to the tender early in the morning, I wanted to go out fishing again. My husband assured me that the fish were all caught and we would be wasting our time. I disagreed. Finally, to shut me up, he laid out the net, and we caught a large haul of fish. Most assuredly, he did not say, "Depart from me, for I am a sinful man." Instead he said, "Now where the hell are we going to sell them; the markets are plugged." He could also have said "Beginner's luck" or "So what, we've had more fish than this before" or any number of other things. Peter's response was unusual, unique in a fishing situation.

The captain on any boat is the final authority on everything that goes on there. Peter was clearly the captain on his boat. The captain bears responsibility for the very lives of others and for the success of the enterprise. After Peter's spectacular confession, Jesus tells him "Do not be afraid; from now on you will be catching people" (Luke 5:10). The transfer of command of the enterprise shifts from Peter to Jesus, its focus from fish to men. The priority will no longer be fish, although fishing does continue in the later portions of the Gospels. The priority will become human encounters.

Jesus in turn can be viewed as thinking like a fisherman in determining the shape of his ministry. He made decisions based on where he would have the most chance of success. He went to the most repressed and poverty-stricken people, those who were ill, demon possessed, on the margins of society. He went to those most affected by the societal upheaval caused by the Roman occupation. He literally went to where the fish were, trying to be at the right place at the right time. Fishermen will go through tremendous privations in hopes of the big catch. Jesus' ministry was a model of a successful fishing strategy: go where the fish are, deploy the right gear at the right time, be skilled at multiple methods of catching fish, be adaptable to suit changing conditions, be willing to calculate odds and take risks. Be willing to risk your life for the big catch. While the fishing culture is half-hidden in the Gospels, it underlies the evangelizing strategy that Jesus employed.

Fish as Food

Just after daybreak, Jesus stood on the beach; but the disciples did not know that it was Jesus. Jesus said to them, "Children, you have no fish, have you?" They answered him, "No." He said to them, "Cast the net to the right side of the boat, and you will find some." So they cast it, and now they were not able to haul it in because there were so many fish. That disciple whom Jesus loved said to Peter, "It is the Lord!" When Simon Peter heard that it was the Lord, he put on some clothes, for he was naked, and jumped into the sea. But the other disciples came in the boat, dragging the net full of fish, for they were not far from the land, only about a hundred yards off. When they had gone ashore, they saw a charcoal fire there, with fish on it, and bread. Jesus said to them, "Bring some of the fish that you have just caught." So Simon Peter went aboard and hauled the net ashore, full of large fish, a hundred fifty-three of them; and though there were so many, the net was not torn. Jesus said to them, "Come and have breakfast." Now none of the disciples dared to ask him, "Who are you?" because they knew it was the Lord. Jesus came and took the bread and gave it to them, and did the same with the fish. This was now the third time that Jesus appeared to the disciples after he was raised from the dead. When they had finished breakfast, Jesus said to Simon Peter, "Simon son of John, do you love me more than these?" He said to him, "Yes, Lord; you know that I love you." Jesus said to him, "Feed my lambs."...   — John 21:4–16

One of the significant experiences in encounters with Jesus throughout the Bible concerns food: feeding others, eating together, hunger, feasting, drinking. The miracle of the loaves and fishes or the feeding of a multitude of people appear several times in various Gospels. The details differ regarding numbers fed, the quantity of loaves and fish, and the amount of left-overs. What fascinates me is the dynamic between Jesus and the fishermen, people whose occupation entailed food production.

In Matthew 14:16 and Mark 6:37, Jesus tells the disciples to give the crowds something to eat, but they balk and he does the job himself. John's version (6:1–14) is somewhat different, but again, it is Jesus who feeds the group. I find it strange that people who fished for a food product and who had their boats nearby in at least a couple of these incidents seem quite incapable of providing anything to eat. One possible conclusion is not that they were unable, but that they were unwilling. Were they in a territory where they were not authorized to fish, and could get in trouble with the Romans? Was it the Sabbath, which could have fostered a clash with religious authorities? Were they simply uncertain of success in a time of fish shortage?

One of the significant experiences in encounters with Jesus throughout the Bible concerns food: feeding others, eating together, hunger, feasting, drinking.

A lengthy passage regarding Jesus as food occurs in John 6:35–70. At the end of Jesus' sermon, many people choose to leave, but the twelve stay. In mariner's terms, this incident can be likened to a mutiny, with the bulk of the crew abandoning ship. The twelve, who include a majority of fishermen, choose not to mutiny. They view themselves as being under command, and they see no other officer under whom they can serve. "Lord, to whom can we go?" (John 6:68) asks Peter. Significantly, Peter does not attempt to retake his own position as captain at this time.

The final chapter of John provides a new turn of events. Jesus asks the fishermen to bring fish to him on the beach, and he commands them to feed others. The significance of the count of fish, 153 in number, and their large size may be symbolic, as numerous writers have surmised.[1] However, it must be mentioned that one of the signs of scarcity in fish populations is a reduction in the size of individual creatures. Large fish are usually a sign of abundance. Over exploitation of fish stocks characteristically leads to diminishing size of the remaining fish. The detail that the fish were large is important, as it supports my premise that regular catches were comprised of fish of small size. I notice that whenever Jesus is present, the catches are large and, in this case, the fish themselves are large, symbolizing God's presence. By implication, catches at other times were of undersized fish in small numbers.

While scholarly opinion tends to hold that chapter 21 is a later addition to this Gospel,[2] I see it as the completing event for the fishermen of Jesus' acquaintance. Its emotional impact increases when it is juxtaposed with the non-canonical Gospel of Peter, chapter 14: "Now it was the last day of Unleavened Bread, and many began to return to their homes since the feast was over. But we, the twelve disciples of the Lord, continued to weep and mourn and each one, still grieving on account of what had happened, left for his own home. But I, Simon Peter, and Andrew, my brother, took our fishing nets and went away to the sea. And with us was Levi, the son of Alphaeus, whom the Lord ... [end of manuscript]."[3]

We do not know how this Gospel ends, but the fragment quoted here indicates the grief that all felt. A comment I often hear from fishermen is that "fishing spoils you for any other job." There is something about the fishing life that is so central to personality and identity that everything else seems second best. A proverb among the Finnish fishermen of the Columbia River states: "Beginning is always difficult, industry overcomes bad luck, and work is our joy."[4] This saying resonates with meaning for fishing peoples everywhere, and it could be applied to the Galilean fishermen. With the death of Jesus and their perception that their work for him had ended, the natural thing for the disciples to do would be to go back to fishing, to the one thing left that provided meaning and solace. But then Jesus appears on the beach. The great catch of fish repeats the experience of the great draught of fish that began their relationship with Jesus as his disciples. Jesus asks Peter three times whether he loves him, and he commands Peter to feed his lambs. Jesus turns over his authority for feeding others to the disciples. He resigns the captaincy once taken from Peter and returns it to him.

The Tax Collector

As Jesus was walking along, he saw a man called Matthew sitting at the tax booth; and he said to him, "Follow me." And he got up and followed him.
— Matt. 9:9

Jesus went out again beside the sea; the whole crowd gathered around him, and he taught them. As he was walking along, he saw Levi son of Alphaeus sitting at the tax booth, and he said to him, "Follow me." And he got up and followed him. And as he sat at dinner in Levi's house, many tax collectors and sinners were also sitting with Jesus and his disciples — for there were many who followed him. When the scribes of the Pharisees saw that he was eating with sinners and tax collectors, they said to his disciples, "Why does he eat with tax collectors and sinners?" When Jesus heard this, he said to them, "Those who are well have no need of a physician, but those who are sick; I have come to call not the righteous but sinners."
— Mark 2:13–17

After this he went out and saw a tax collector named Levi, sitting at the tax booth; and he said to him, "Follow me." And he got up, left everything, and followed him. Then Levi gave a great banquet for him in his house; and there was a large crowd of tax collectors and others sitting at the table with them. The Pharisees and their scribes were complaining to his disciples, saying, "Why do you eat and drink with tax collectors and sinners?" Jesus answered, "Those who are well have no need of a physician, but those who are sick; I have come to call not the righteous but sinners to repentance." — Luke 5:27–32

The Bible lists Matthew (Levi) as a tax collector, a loaded term implying greed, corruption, and sinfulness, as he handled Roman money that bore graven images in the likenesses of various emperors. Yet Jesus called him as a disciple, and there is no biblical evidence that Matthew did not get along with the other disciples, unlike Judas. Matthew, however, had fishing connections that are not evident in scripture, which may have made him a familiar figure to the other followers. A brief description of the taxation system imposed by the Roman government on the fishing industry corroborates this claim.

According to W. H. Wuellner, after the Roman occupation of the Middle East, the area's rising population and urbanization created an increasing demand for food.[1] The Romans sought to organize fisheries and achieve greater economic efficiency through the centralization of fishing activities and encouragement of larger scale fishing enterprises. These new fishing methods required larger capital investments to achieve profitability. The tax collectors had the capital to lend to promote expansion of the fisheries. Matthew's role as a tax collector implies wealth and the ability to lend money. He represents a potential source of funding for fishermen such as Zebedee, James and John, and Peter and Andrew, much as a local bank funds capital purchases by a business today.

Two systems of fishing licensing appear to be in place in the first century. "Royal fishermen" delivered specific amounts of fish at certain times to a royal household or temple, and were paid in cash or in kind. In "tax fishing" fishermen leased fishing rights from a tax collector, an official under contract with the Roman administration. Such fishermen usually worked with a partner and had a contract that required them to pay a fish tax on each catch but permitted them subsequently to trade in the local market for their own profit.[2] Matthew was such a tax gatherer in Capernaum (Matt. 9:9). Capernaum was strategically located near the border of the lands ruled by Philip and Herod, so a customs office was situated there, as well as a small garrison of Roman guards. Matthew's position made him part of the fishing infrastructure of the place, with business connections with fishermen.

A tradition that surfaces frequently alludes to Zebedee's family connections with the Temple in Jerusalem as purveyor of fish to the High Priest's family.[3] According to scripture, Zebedee hired a number of fishermen to work with him, in addition to having his sons on board. We know his sons as James and John; the hired men remain forever anonymous. This example illustrates two distinct groups of fishermen. The first group owned their own boats and gear; the second had no stake in vessel or fishing equipment. The Bible hints at the method of crew payment in a passage that notes that each catch was counted after it was landed, which would have served the purpose of determining its value both for taxation and for crew wages.[4] This custom persists today among many of the world's fisheries, as it is common to pay crew a share of the catch. My husband and I do it ourselves, paying a percentage of the value of the catch to each crew member, a system recognized in the U.S. tax code. Matthew's role as tax collector also implies his role as an accountant; he would be intimately familiar with each boat's catch and the wages due each fisher.

As tax collector and fish licenser Matthew was in the position of a patron to the fishermen. Patron-client relationships were an important feature of Mediterranean cultures and introduce some complexity into the relations between Matthew and the fishermen.[5] In biblical writings and in modern times, tax collectors win no popularity contests. However, the relationship between Matthew and the fishermen may not have been negative. As an intermediary between fishermen and the Roman authorities, he may have been in a position to provide them some protection. I imagine a conversation between Matthew and a Roman official might have gone something like this: "Lucius, I need to talk with you about the fishing situation. I know revenues are down, but I also know these guys, and they haven't been catching much. They're not lazy. They're working as hard as they can. The fish just aren't there. Can you go easy on them this year? They're all highliners, but it's just a terrible year. I've been in this trade twenty years, and I've never seen it so bleak. Tax them too much and it will wipe them out. You know they've been selling the bulk of their catches to the garrison at pretty reasonable prices, even though the Jerusalem Temple is screaming for more fish. It's a shortage, and any break you can give them would be appreciated."

Matthew could also have had a patron-client relationship with people who manufactured twine, with boat carpenters, or with fish processors. Did he extend credit? Did he own the boats or the gear? Were his boats in competition with lineage-owned boats, such as that of Zebedee and his sons? Many possibilities exist for complex relationships between Matthew and the fishermen, but there most certainly must have been a relationship.

Yet another role for Matthew might have been as fish broker. In the economically risky world of fisheries, where each catch generates a race to market with a highly perishable product, fishermen may rely on brokers to sell fish for them while they continue with the fishing operation. Fishermen's wives frequently take on this role, especially in artisanal fisheries. The Roman garrison in Capernaum may have provided a lucrative market for fish. It would make sense for fishermen to concentrate on fishing and rely on an intermediary to assist in the fish marketing, especially with gentiles. Alternative markets such as the Temple in Jerusalem and at Mediterranean port cities such as Tyre and Sidon, with their connections to other parts of the Roman Empire, might also have presented attractive opportunities where a broker's expertise would have garnered greater monetary returns. However, the fishermen risked the danger of exploitation by such a broker.

There are many "mays" and "mights" in this passage about Matthew, and many questions remain unanswered. I find no pejorative words about Matthew in the Gospels except the stereotyping of his role as a tax collector. Including him as part of the inner circle of the disciples was unusual because of their status difference, he as patron and they as clients, rather than because of his occupation. His place among the twelve introduces complexity into their relationships, and brings the Roman Empire very near their little group.

The One Who Isn't There

But Judas Iscariot, one of his disciples (the one who was about to betray him), said, "Why was this perfume not sold for three hundred denarii and the money given to the poor?" (He said this not because he cared about the poor, but because he was a thief; he kept the common purse and used to steal what was put into it.) — John 12:4–6

Fishermen learn by observation and inference. Observation includes looking for what is not there. Applying this method to the Bible, what is not in the texts may be as important as what is there. I looked for Judas in

I confess to having a sneaking sympathy for Judas, always the outsider, never completely part of the group.

the fishing and boating scenes, to find out how he related to the other disciples. He is not there. He appears in the last supper, in some of the traveling scenes, at Lazarus' home in Bethany, and in connection with Jesus' betrayal. He is apparently the treasurer of Jesus' group. But he does not fish.

Background reading suggests that Judas came from Kerioth, a village in southern Judea.[1] John's Gospel (12:6) forthrightly labels Judas a thief who stole from the money box and did not care for the poor. Who was Judas and why did he have control of the purse strings? Because of his origin, which was not Galilee, he was not part of the fishing community. To the fishermen he would have been an outsider. He would have been seen as an unproductive person, since he did not fish. However, he also would have been a neutral person to whom they entrusted their money, as he did not have the business entanglements and partnerships that the fishermen did, nor was he connected with taxation, as Matthew was.

Fishermen learn by observation and inference.
Observation includes looking for what is not there.

If their fishing money was supplying the needs of the group, they may have wanted an uninvolved person to handle the cash, to avoid competitive rivalries as to who was contributing how much, based on better catches. Fishermen's associations are notorious for leadership difficulties. Their members' egalitarian ethic pressures them not to volunteer for a position that will single them out in any way. The job of treasurer is the job no one wants, as it gives the person selected intimate knowledge of the competition's finances, a potent source of conflict.

I confess to having a sneaking sympathy for Judas, always the outsider, never completely part of the group. The social dynamics of his situation in a group dominated by adherents of the fishing occupation meant he could never share complete intimacy with them. Even the role that he assumed brought him into conflict with the others. While John's Gospel claims that Judas stole money, such accusations were the inevitable outcome of the position he was in. Win-win was never a possibility for Judas.

Women in Fishing

Jesus left that place and went away to the district of Tyre and Sidon. Just then a Canaanite woman from that region came out and started shouting, "Have mercy on me, Lord, Son of David; my daughter is tormented by a demon." But he did not answer her at all. And his disciples came and urged him, saying, "Send her away, for she keeps shouting after us." He answered, "I was sent only to the lost sheep of the house of Israel." But she came and knelt before him, saying, "Lord, help me." He answered, "It is not fair to take the children's food and throw it to the dogs." She said, "Yes, Lord, yet even the dogs eat the crumbs that fall from their masters' table." — Matt. 15:21–28

From there he set out and went away to the region of Tyre. He entered a house and did not want anyone to know he was there. Yet he could not escape notice, but a woman whose little daughter had an unclean spirit immediately

108

heard about him, and she came and bowed down at his feet. Now the woman was a Gentile, of Syrophoenician origin. She begged him to cast the demon out of her daughter. He said to her, "Let the children be fed first, for it is not fair to take the children's food and throw it to the dogs." But she answered him, "Sir, even the dogs under the table eat the children's crumbs." Then he said to her, "For saying that, you may go — the demon has left your daughter." So she went home, found the child lying on the bed, and the demon gone.   — Mark 7:24–30

Maritime anthropology stresses that a feature of fishing communities is the degree of autonomy and decision-making leeway that women have, due to the absence of the community's males for extended periods of time.[1] Clarification of women's roles in fishing cultures is a relatively recent topic of academic research.[2] In many countries women now own and operate vessels, keep the books and manage fishing operations. More traditional roles include processing and marketing of fish and preparation of gear. On the Columbia River, for example, in the nineteenth century, many men preferred nets knit by women, owing to their superior workmanship.[3] Georgia Maki, who earned her living by mending nets, said, "Other women used to knit the floaters [a type of gillnet] ... different ones have mentioned it, their mother or their grandmother or somebody did it."[4] Since spinning was women's work in both biblical times and into the twentieth century in Middle Eastern cultures,[5] women must have produced the linen thread used for nets. Did they also knit the web, or sew the nets together? Did they weave the fabric used for sails, or was this a purchased specialty item? Were they able to earn an independent income with these skills?

Zebedee's wife exhibited the independent characteristics of a fishing wife when she pushed her sons forward as deserving preferment in Jesus' future kingdom.

Fish processing by cleaning and salting them or preserving them in some fashion is often the domain of women, particularly when the men are occupied with catching the fish. This is part of the customary division of labor in a family-owned fishing enterprise. An astonishing variety of fish products existed in the Mediterranean region including pickled, brine cured, dried and salted, or smoked fish, fish rendered into oil for lamps or for medicinal purposes, dyes from the murex snail, and fermented fish sauces that were shipped in amphorae throughout the Roman Empire.[6] While some of these products required manufacturing skills possessed only by a skilled artisan, undoubtedly many of them were prepared by women. Maritime cultures worldwide have and still do employ female labor for fish processing. For example, the great salt cod trade of Newfoundland relied extensively on women's labor well into the twentieth century, especially in preparing and drying the cod from the inshore fishery. Women made up part of the cannery crews in the North American salmon and tuna canning industry of the nineteenth and twentieth centuries and were particularly adept at filling the cans by hand.

Marketing, too, can be a woman's occupation. Recent research by Patricia Dutcher-Walls, professor of Old Testament and Hebrew Scripture at Knox College in Toronto, found a great deal of similarity between rural villages in today's developing world and Israelite communities from 1200 B.C.E. to 200 C.E. She said, "When women in today's peasant communities take their products to market, they have an income that isn't reliant on a husband or village elder. There is every reason to believe that the same situation existed for some of the women of the Bible."[7] I would go further and name names: Mary Magdalene, Lydia, and the Syrophoenician woman.

Consider the example of the Syrophoenician woman. The gentile and Phoenician parts of her ethnic identity, plus her residency in a coastal, maritime community, lead to the possibility that she came from a maritime background. The sparring that took place between her and Jesus demonstrates an independence of thought of a woman in the maritime trades. Further, it is she and not a male of her household (assuming there was one) who requests the casting out of an unclean spirit from her daughter. Contrast this incident with the raising of Jairus's daughter, the healing of the centurion's servant, or the epileptic child in Mark 9:14–29. All the requests are made by males. Nor is the woman put off by Jesus' remark that his priority is the Jewish community. Rather, she insisted on a place if not at the table then under it. The story of the Syrophoenician woman operates on more than one level. It is a healing story and a story of faith, but it is also a story of egalitarianism and independence characteristic of a maritime community.

Maritime anthropology stresses that a feature of fishing communities is the degree of autonomy and decision-making leeway that women have, due to the absence of the community's males for extended periods of time.

Zebedee's wife exhibited the independent characteristics of a fishing wife when she pushed her sons forward as deserving preferment in Jesus' future kingdom (Matt. 20:20–27). She involved herself in their careers as his followers, and may have played some sort of role in the fishing operation, perhaps preparing or marketing the catch. Peter's mother-in-law, and by implication his wife, are two other female figures connected with the fishermen disciples who are known mainly for their role of hospitality (Luke 5:39). Providing food and a place for fishermen to socialize can serve an important function in a fishing community even now, as fishermen frequently gather at a central home to discuss the issues of the day.

Excavations in the city of Capernaum have recovered a house that some archaeologists claim to be that of Peter. Tradition also indicates that it was Peter's home, and that it was used as an early place of worship as a "house church."[8] That Peter was a leader among fishermen was obvious; that his home was a central gathering place and his wife and mother-in-law were the ones that made it possible is part of the hidden fishing code of the Bible.

An Independent Woman

The twelve were with him, as well as some women who had been cured of evil spirits and infirmities: Mary, called Magdalene, from whom seven demons had gone out, and Joanna, the wife of Herod's steward Chuza, and Susanna, and many others, who provided for them out of their resources.   — Luke 8:1–3

Mary Magdalene came from a Galilean fishing town. She was a major influential personage in the lives of Jesus and his disciples. Given that her home town of Magdala was famed for its preserved fish, I have wondered whether she had any connection with the processing or marketing of this product, a customary occupation for women in fishing communities.

Due to some confusion regarding the various Marys in the Gospels, legends and church traditions frequently depict her as a whore. The freedom with which she mixed with Jesus' companions indicates to me that she had the kind of independence expected of maritime women in fishing communities, which contrasted sharply with female roles in other types of

114

communities. She appears to have had an independent income with which she supported Jesus' ministry.[1] Such an income is readily explicable if she took part in fish processing or marketing.

The freedom with which she mixed with Jesus' companions indicates to me that she had the kind of independence expected of maritime women in fishing communities, which contrasted sharply with female roles in other types of communities.

Legends from the south of France recount that after Jesus' death Mary Magdalene was set adrift with several companions in the Mediterranean, in a boat without sails or oars. They landed in Provence, where she and the others preached the Gospel. Paintings and bas reliefs in churches in the south of France depict her preaching to the fishing fleet in Marseilles.[2]

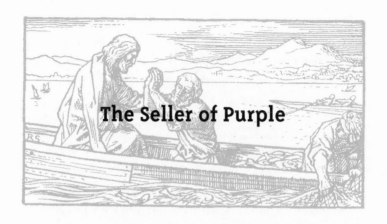

The Seller of Purple

[We came to] Philippi, which is a leading city of the district of Macedonia and a Roman colony. We remained in this city for some days. On the sabbath day we went outside the gate by the river, where we supposed there was a place of prayer; and we sat down and spoke to the women who had gathered there. A certain woman named Lydia, a worshiper of God, was listening to us; she was from the city of Thyatira and a dealer in purple cloth. The Lord opened her heart to listen eagerly to what was said by Paul. When she and her household were baptized, she urged us, saying, "If you have judged me to be faithful to the Lord, come and stay at my home." And she prevailed upon us.   — Acts 16:12–15

Lydia is an example of a woman of independent means associated with a maritime trade. She was a native of Thyatira, located in a region of Asia Minor known as Lydia. An inscription found in Thyatira provides evidence of the presence of a dyer's guild. The second chapter of Revelation contains a letter to the church at Thyatira. Good roads connected the town with coastal cities. Philippi, where Lydia lived, was a city in eastern Macedonia, on the east-west Egnation Highway between Rome and Asia, allowing her ready contacts with both suppliers and markets.[1] Philippi appears to have had significant contact with a number of the Roman emperors and empresses, for whom the color purple was a symbol of rank.[2]

To piece this story together, it is necessary to discuss Lydia's trade, that of a seller of purple. The word "purple" referred both to purple dye and to purple dyed cloth. The dye itself came from a saltwater snail, the murex, found in the eastern Mediterranean. Dye works were ubiquitous along the Phoenician shore, especially in such cities as Ugarit, Dor, Tyre, and Sidon. The word "Phoenician" comes from *phoinix,* meaning reddish or purple. Phoenicia, which included the coastal areas of Syria, Lebanon, and Israel, was, therefore, the "land of purple." Tyre in particular produced high-quality dyes, noted for being colorfast. The Roman emperors favored Tyrian purple above all others. Tyre was also noted for the odor that emanated from the dye works, despite being located upwind from the prevailing winds.[3] In ancient Israel, the tribe of Zebulun, located on the northeast coast of the Mediterranean, had exclusive rights to the murex fishery.[4]

In her position as a seller of purple, numerous questions arise about Lydia. Was she a middleman between the snail fishers, the dye workers, and the cloth producers? Did she deal in the dye itself, or the purple cloth, or both? Did she have fishermen working for her, so that she could sell their product to others, acting as their patron? Did the fishers or their family members also produce the dye? Did she import from the eastern Mediterranean cities such as Sidon, Tyre and others and sell to the imperial cults at Philippi, or ship dye to her original home city of Thyatira? The combinations of possibilities are endless, and we can never know with certainty the exact details of her position in this trade. What we can surmise is that she was a wealthy and successful woman, probably unmarried or widowed, who owned her own house in Philippi, had had some contact with Jewish religious practice, and had extensive contacts in her business, due to its maritime nature.

Paul met Lydia and a number of other women worshipping the one God of the Jews outside Philippi on the river bank of the Gingite (modern Angista). Curiously, there is no archaeological evidence that Philippi ever had a Jewish population.[5] However, Thyatira did.[6] Did Lydia learn of the one God in Thyatira? Or through her clients and contacts along the Mediterranean coast, perhaps from Tyre and Sidon, whose waterfront communities had Jewish and early Christian communities? Lydia became the first European convert to Christianity and invited, actually insisted, that Paul and his companions use her home in Philippi as their base of operation. Implied in this story is that Paul and his fellow evangelists entered into a sort of patron-client relationship with Lydia, entering her house and staying there under her protection, and using her home as the local church.

What we can surmise is that she was a wealthy and successful woman... and had extensive contacts in her business, due to its maritime nature.

Paul baptized Lydia "and her household," which indicates her role as a patron of other clients who would have been considered part of her household. Women played an important role in the Roman cults at Philippi. Women also played an important role in the church in Philippi and Thyatira, according to scripture.[7] We do not know what happened to Lydia, but we can imagine that the prominence of her position, her sponsorship of the church, and her business contacts all enhanced Paul's mission and the planting of the first European church.

Fishing Rights

He said to them, "Come away to a deserted place all by yourselves and rest a while." For many were coming and going, and they had no leisure even to eat. And they went away in the boat to a deserted place by themselves. Now many saw them going and recognized them, and they hurried there on foot from all the towns and arrived ahead of them.   — Mark 6:31–33

In fishing communities, access to fisheries resources is crucial. Numerous descriptions exist in marine anthropological literature of community systems of organization to access fish.[1] Such community systems of rules, customs, and territories are ubiquitous, so the United Nations Food and Agricultural Organization coined an acronym for them: TURFs, territorial use rights in fisheries. TURFs may be defined as "community-held rights of use (or tenure) and exclusion over the fishery resources within a specific area and for a period of time. Accompanying these rights might be certain responsibilities for maintenance and proper management of the resource base, as well as restrictions on the exercise of the rights of use and exclusion."[2]

Archaeological finds in both Bethsaida and Capernaum include fishing implements such as lead net weights, both sail-making and net-making needles, sinkers, stone anchors, fishhooks, and a fisherman's seal depicting two men in a fish boat throwing out a cast net.

As an example, on the Columbia River where my husband Kent and I fish, such TURFs are known as drift rights. Fishermen band together to clear snags such as old tree stumps and other debris that might tear their nets from the bottom of the river. The group then has the primary right to fish in that area or "drift," to the exclusion of outside fishermen who have not assisted with clearing snags. A system of rules drawn up by the fishermen's group governs each area, in order to minimize conflict with competing boats. As one fisherman put it succinctly: "Drift rights are a gentlemen's agreement, but you've got to have a way to deal with the folks who aren't gentlemen."[3] Fishing communities around the world have organized their access to fishing grounds by such means for thousands of years.

Not only do fishermen in a community fish together, they also tend to socialize with each other, and they may be related. Sharing vital fishing knowledge of obstructions such as rocks and snags, stages of the tide that may be productive, and weather conditions is a daily event in family and community interaction. Children become aware at an early age of the need to learn a great deal of local data in order to be successful at the fishery. The locations of safe anchorages, of reefs, eddies, and backwaters that harbor fish searching for food, of underwater springs that provide water that attracts fish, are all part of the knowledge base that fishermen amass during the course of their lives. The scripture passage that begins this chapter indicates that the habits and haunts of the fishing disciples were so well known to their fellow citizens that they could predict where they were going with Jesus for some quiet time and beat them to the spot.

Four Galilean fishing communities of biblical fame were Capernaum, Bethsaida, Magdala, and Gergesa, also called Gadara. Capernaum was located on an important trade route between the Mediterranean ports and the territory east of the Sea of Galilee. As George Adams Smith so aptly put it: "Judea was on the road to nowhere; Galilee is covered with roads to everywhere — roads from the harbours of the Phoenician coast to Samaria, Gilead, Hauran and Damascus; roads from Sharon to the valley of the Jordan; roads from the sea to the desert; roads from Egypt to Assyria."[4] Not only was Galilee crisscrossed with highways, but the Sea of Galilee itself was a medium for transportation frequently alluded to in the Bible. In New Testament times, the fishing villages of Bethsaida, Magdala, and Capernaum were all readily reachable by water. Gergesa, also known as Gadara, where the miracle of the Gadarene swine took place, had a sophisticated fishing port, complete with tanks of plastered stone for keeping live fish.[5]

Not only do fishermen in a community fish together, they also tend to socialize with each other, and they may be related.

Jesus recruited Peter, Andrew, James, and John from Capernaum, where Peter had a house, although he was born in Bethsaida, as were Andrew and Philip. Archaeological finds in both Bethsaida and Capernaum include fishing implements such as lead net weights, both sail-making and net-making needles, sinkers, stone anchors, fishhooks, and a fisherman's seal depicting two men in a fish boat throwing out a cast net. Magdala, home of Mary Magdalene, is also the site of the discovery of an early net needle.[6] Material evidence indicates a fishing industry of artisanal fishermen who worked out of small wooden boats powered by sail or oar or both. They utilized a variety of technologies including nets of various kinds and hook and line.

The *Encyclopaedia Judaica* refers to numerous *halakhot* (law) and *aggadot* (lore) about fishing and fishermen in the Babylonian and Jerusalem Talmuds. Fish were considered ownerless property; whoever caught them had the right to keep them. This in theory applied even to fish already netted, as long as the net had not been taken out of the water. However, the rabbis ruled that "in the interests of peace" the fish belonged to the owners of the net.[7] We know from the Bible that fishermen sorted their catch into "clean" and "unclean" categories at the end of each fishing period, an example of a practice specific to their religious tradition.

Mendel Nun tells us that in the Old Testament, commercial fishing rights were given to the tribe of Naphtali by Joshua Bin Nun (Son of the Fish), although angling was open to all tribes.[8] He also noted that Tabgha, a well-known fishing ground near Capernaum, apparently required fishermen to work in partnership with two boats up until modern times because of the limited area of the grounds.[9] We know from the New

Testament that Peter and Andrew owned a boat and were in partnership with Zebedee, James and John, who also owned a boat, and that they fished in this area, thus demonstrating an early pattern of this partnering custom. Seining sites were limited, due to the need to have an area free of obstructions and rocks, which explains Nun's description of the seining crew sailing off to "catch a good fishing area."[10] Access was critical to ensure fishing success.

These few clues provide us with a sense of the system of norms and customs for fishing on the Sea of Galilee. Religious and community influence, access to resources, the topography of the fishing grounds, the type of gear used, and intimate knowledge of the locale gained from experience and oral tradition governed fishing practices. The fishermen around the shoreline formed a society uniquely adapted to extract a living from the resources the lake had to offer, based on custom and generations of experience. At a minimum, the Roman occupation challenged their norms and customs, reduced their chances of financial success, and affected their emotional well-being.

The Thin Places

The Pharisees and Sadducees came, and to test Jesus they asked him to show them a sign from heaven. He answered them, "When it is evening, you say, 'It will be fair weather, for the sky is red.' And in the morning, 'It will be stormy today, for the sky is red and threatening.' You know how to interpret the appearance of the sky, but you cannot interpret the signs of the times. An evil and adulterous generation asks for a sign, but no sign will be given to it except the sign of Jonah." Then he left them and went away.

— Matt. 16:1–4

The Celts referred to "the thin places," those places where the intersection of the world of God and the world of humans is very near, and boundaries are insubstantial. For me, the Sea of Galilee in the time of Jesus qualifies as one of the thin places.[1] I am always searching for authenticity, for the detail that shows that a fisherman's mind is present or that a maritime world view has shaped a description of an event. Jesus' comment about knowing the signs of the weather was a fisherman's observation, punctuated by

126

reference to the fish story of Jonah and the whale. When these details occur in scripture, the boundaries that divide us from God dissolve, and we are very near to the time when Jesus sailed on the lake with his friends.

At one time I envisaged categorizing the passages regarding fishing and fishermen into either incidents or miracles, but the borders between these two terms was more fluid than I realized. In attempting to divide the real and everyday from the miraculous, based on how fishing people view the natural world, I discovered the paradox that the natural world is itself miraculous. The fishing stories, the intersection of the lives of fish in their water world and the lives of human beings, show God working through natural processes. The fishing disciples recognized God working in the material world, and saw Jesus as God's incarnation precisely because he took part in the natural and social world they were so familiar with. Trying to identify miraculous events makes defining the boundaries between the natural and supernatural a frustrating exercise.

What may be a miracle for some is not necessarily a miracle for me. The King James version of the Bible headlines chapter 5 of Matthew's Gospel with the title "Draft of Fishes and Other Miracles." I think this label has misled countless generations. I have never been able to bring myself to count a large catch of fish as a miracle, nor would the fishermen of my acquaintance. It's a wonderful event that occasionally happens, but there is usually a good reason for it. A wind change, a weather change, or any number of other variables may contribute to a spectacular haul. I also think of Jesus' appearance as a ghost to the disciples during the storm at sea as a natural phenomenon known as St. Elmo's fire, long associated with seamen's stories of ghosts and spirits. This electrical charge appears as a light on masts and other high places. Italian fishermen call it *Corpo Santo* (the holy body) or *corpusante,* after Saint Erasmus or Elmo, patron saint of sailors. White or bluish flames, sometimes accompanied by a crackling or hissing noise, appear, usually toward the end of a storm. The flames do not give off heat nor do they burn anything. There is some conjecture that the burning bush that Moses saw may have been a form of St. Elmo's fire, such as Mountain Top Luminescence, a related phenomenon. Because of the propensity for *corpusante* to appear at the end of storms, mariners generally consider it a good omen, as it heralds the end of bad weather.[2]

The differences in perception and knowledge between ourselves and the people and events of the first century C.E. make it difficult to ascertain the physical facts behind each miraculous event. Our forebears were more closely aligned with magic, myth, fable, and miracle than we are. But I can say that something happened, and it resulted in a radical change in the people closest to the event. They identified the event as being God-inspired. Whatever happened drew them closer to Jesus whom they identified with God.

The fishing disciples recognized God working in the material world, and saw Jesus as God's incarnation precisely because he took part in the natural and social world they were so familiar with.

The miracle of turning water into wine at the wedding in Cana is often considered to be a blessing of the institution of marriage, or a foretaste of the Last Supper. Baptismal symbolism is rich too. Scripture tells us that Jesus and his fishing disciples were present at the wedding. Typically, a wedding feast lasted several days. No exact number of guests could be forecast, making it difficult to predict how much food and drink to provide.[3] When the host appears to be running out of wine, Mary tells Jesus of their plight. And water transforms into wine.

I think of this as a fishermen's miracle. If we think in terms of scarcity and abundance, the poverty implied in running out of wine at a wedding was overcome by the supply that Jesus provided. The familiar water of the fishermen's everyday lives was the medium they worked on and in which their prey lived. It transformed into wine, wonderful wine, in lavish quantity. I believe that behind the story of the events at Cana is the disciples' recognition of the central place that Jesus was about to assume in their lives. They saw the possibility that their humdrum fishery, beleaguered by the Romans and beset with problems, could become the base for a transformation to a just and equitable society, "the kingdom of God." What I consider to be the miracles of the Gospels are the conversion experiences, the change of heart exhibited by Peter and others, when Jesus entered the fishing world.

The Hiding Place

"Again, the kingdom of heaven is like a merchant in search of fine pearls; on finding one pearl of great value, he went and sold all that he had and bought it.

"Again, the kingdom of heaven is like a net that was thrown into the sea and caught fish of every kind; when it was full, they drew it ashore, sat down, and put the good into baskets but threw out the bad. So it will be at the end of the age. The angels will come out and separate the evil from the righteous and throw them into the furnace of fire, where there will be weeping and gnashing of teeth."

— Matt. 13:45–50

Both of the opening parables incorporate fishing technology and imagery. Jesus likens the kingdom of heaven to a "net [*sagene,* or seine] that was thrown into the sea and caught fish of every kind" (Matt. 13:47), which are then sorted through, the good kept and the bad thrown away. He also likens the kingdom to a valuable pearl, bought by a merchant for a fabulous price. The context for these stories is that Jesus has been preaching to crowds, speaking to them in a series of parables that are mainly agricultural in theme. When he retires for the day, the disciples ask him to explain, as they have not grasped his meaning. In his first explanatory parable, he continues the agricultural theme. However, the next two parables concern maritime experience: the pearl of great price and the kingdom of heaven being like a net. Matthew's position as businessman, tax gatherer, customs official, and fish licenser would have drawn him to the story of the pearl. Given their understanding of fish marketing, the story of a marine product, a pearl, would have made sense to the fishermen. This story is more accessible to the modern-day reader too.

For us to understand the story of the net, more background is needed. It is truly surprising what can come up in a net! Anyone who watched the movie *Forrest Gump* will recall the trash and debris that surfaced in his shrimp trawl. A Columbia River fisherman who spent years diving to clear obstructions from fishing grounds described his experience: "You know, the river's a good place to hide anything. We've got ship's anchors, TV antennas, refrigerators, freezers, stoves, but mostly logs.... And we've pulled old seining barges ... seining houses, scows and one drift in

Vancouver got a steam engine, 16 ton steam engine off their drift."[1]

In Galilee it is common to bring up rocks in nets.[2] Sorting involves removing debris as well as fish from the net, and then separating the fish that are good to eat from those that are inedible, as well as separating kosher from non-kosher fish. Nun mentions that occasionally water serpents come up in the net along with the fish.[3] Did this bycatch lead to Jesus' question in Matthew 7:9–10, "Is there anyone among you who, if your child asks for bread, will give a stone? Or if the child asks for a fish, will give a snake?"

The catch could be eaten fresh, smoked, pickled, salted, or dried.[4] Fish sauces were popular throughout the Roman Empire.[5] Not only was the catch sorted to eliminate undesirable or unmarketable creatures, sorting helped ensure that the fish most suited to fresh consumption could be marketed immediately, as contrasted with those to be preserved, which were set aside. The catch was counted in order to permit division of the profits among the partners and for taxation purposes. When Jesus talks of sorting the catch, he is involving the disciples' daily experience, in effect saying, "This is what the kingdom of God is like. It is like a seine that catches everything. The catch will be sorted, and the good fish preserved. That which is not useful will be thrown away."

A different take on this parable occurs in the non-canonical Gospel of Thomas, paragraph 8: "And he said, 'The human one is like a wise fisherman, who cast his net [*amphlibestron*] into the sea and drew it up from the sea full of little fish. Among them the wise fisherman discovered a fine large fish. He threw all the little fish back into the sea, and easily chose the large fish. Anyone here with two good ears had better listen.' "[6]

The story of the seine reminds me that God is fishing for everyone and relying on a crew, that is disciples, to help him do it.

Is this an invitation to choose among the gods, to reject the statues, cultic figures, and mythological deities and choose Jesus as the big fish, echoing Tertullian? While scholarly circles have tried to demonstrate that these two stories stem from a common root, the Greek indicates that the nets employed in each are different. One is a seine, one a cast net, indicating to me that each author intended a different meaning.[7] In my mind, the timing, the methodology and the catch sorting component of the two stories are quite different. The seine relies on teamwork among multiple crew members, and it is a slower paced operation than the sudden throw of the cast net. The catch of the two will be quite different in size, with the seine capable of capturing far more fish than the cast net.

The story of the seine reminds me that God is fishing for everyone and relying on a crew, that is disciples, to help him do it. The tale suggests that it is possible for everyone to be part of the kingdom and that God is deliberate in his pace, but God ultimately will sort out good from evil. On the other hand, the story of the cast net hints at a God who is sudden to act, who acts alone, and who intends the kingdom for only a small group. The tales indicate two very different views of God that Christians still struggle with.

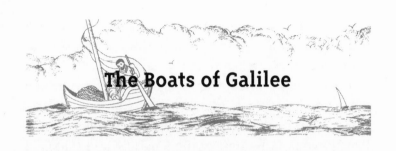

The Boats of Galilee

Again he began to teach beside the sea. Such a very large
crowd gathered around him that he got into a boat on the
sea and sat there, while the whole crowd was beside the
sea on the land.   — Mark 4:1

Jesus fished with his disciples in their boats. He also
used the vessels for traveling, and, as the above scripture tells us, as a pulpit. The late twentieth-century
discovery of a first-century fishing boat in the mud of
the Sea of Galilee has led to wide publicity and hy-
perbolic claims, including the nickname, the "Jesus
boat." Found near Magdala, it measures approximately
26½ feet long by 7½ feet wide and 4½ feet high. The
builder used cedar planking and oak frames. Sidar,
Aleppo pine, hawthorn, willow, and redbud are also
in evidence, woods that are less commonly used, and
which would be considered inferior boat lumber. Some
of the wood was salvaged from other discarded vessels and recycled in the construction of this boat. At
least two other boats lay nearby, indicating a possible
ship graveyard where old boats were junked out and

used for spare parts. Alternatively, they may have been part of the remains of the fleet that sank in the Battle of Migdal.[1]

Salvaging various kinds of woods for use in boat construction or repair is a fairly typical adaptation worldwide when faced with a shortage of good timber or a need to economize. Removing boat parts can be hard work, undertaken only when necessity dictates. When we constructed our Columbia River boat, the *Floozie,* we used scraps of ironbark left over from previous boat-building projects, since it was difficult to obtain this particular type of wood. Our boat originally had oak timbers and cedar planking. We used yew wood ribs to repair it some years later, as good oak was very hard to come by at the time, and we had a plentiful supply of yew.

When I compare the Galilee boat with our own, I am struck by the similarities.

A boat the size of the Galilee boat could accommodate a crew of four to seven, with sails or oars used for power, and a larger oar or sweep used for steering. The boat could be used for fishing and for transportation purposes, possibly taking passengers or an occasional load of freight to other ports on the lake. A cooking pot and a lamp found adjacent to the vessel in its archaeological site indicate possible items in its complement of necessary supplies for prosecuting the fishery. Other necessary equipment would have included ropes, a stone anchor or two, fishing nets for work periods, sail and net mending tools, and possibly tools for emergency boat repairs. A knife or two, a club for killing the occasional unwanted serpent, and a gaff or possibly a grapple hook might also have formed part of the boat's equipment.

The boat did not exist in a vacuum. It was the largest and most expensive tool that the fishing disciples possessed.

When I compare the Galilee boat with our own, I am struck by the similarities. Our Columbia River boat is also wood, about 28 feet long, beamier than the ancient vessel, with oak frames and cedar planking similar to that used in the Galilee boat. Although the oak and cedar species may be different, the reason for using these woods is the same. Oak is tough, but when steamed it will bend to form ribs. Cedar planking is durable, and resists rot. The combination is hard to beat. Although our boat is powered by a gasoline engine, there was a time when sail and oar were all that were available here, too. A century ago, my husband's great-grandfather, also a fisherman, was known as a particularly good sailor, able to maximize the wind's ability to push his boat along in the Columbia River estuary.

I wonder about the specific skills the various fishing disciples had that enabled their partnerships to work. Who was the best sailor? Who was best at mending or developing gear? Was there one who was particularly adept at boat repairs? At sail mending? Who had the best sense of where the fish were at any given time? Who dealt with disagreements and kept day-to-day operations running smoothly? And who was the cook? All of these skills were needed to make the boat and the fishing operation work. The boat did not exist in a vacuum. It was the largest and most expensive tool that the fishing disciples possessed. But it was a tool that depended on the combined skills of captain and crew to achieve maximum effectiveness. Yet were it not for the archaeological discovery of the Galilee boat, we would know even less about the vessels employed by the fishermen on the Sea of Galilee than we do about their nets.

Market Centers

Jesus departed with his disciples to the sea, and a great multitude from Galilee followed him; hearing all that he was doing, they came to him in great numbers from Judea, Jerusalem, Idumea, beyond the Jordan, and the region around Tyre and Sidon.   — Mark 3:7–8

He came down with them and stood on a level place, with a great crowd of his disciples and a great multitude of people from all Judea, Jerusalem, and the coast of Tyre and Sidon.   — Luke 6:17

The Roman Empire at the time of Jesus provided protection to an extensive and active trading network. The empire's need for grain and other foodstuffs, including salt and pickled fish, in enormous quantities, encouraged the development of fast-moving vessels that could move large quantities of goods from the eastern part of the Mediterranean Sea to Rome and her colonies. Reviewing the list of fishing artifacts found at various archaeological sites on the Sea of Galilee reveals such items as a bronze needle for net mending, lead weights, iron nails, pitch for caulking boats, web, rope, sail needles, and hooks, a wide variety of goods. It would be unrealistic to conclude that fishermen manufactured all of these disparate items themselves or even that they were all manufactured locally. The fishery on the Sea of Galilee was relatively small and localized. It might not have been large enough to support such specialized industries as the manufacture of bronze needles. Purchasing or trading for the supplies needed to prosecute the fishing trade must have been part of the disciples' seasonal round. Fishermen could have obtained such articles in maritime-oriented locales like Tyre and Sidon.

Easily reachable from Galilee by excellent trade routes, Tyre and Sidon were famous in ancient times for the multiplicity of goods available in their markets. The twenty-seventh chapter of Ezekiel lists the astonishing array of merchandise that passed through Tyre and made it wealthy. By segregating from that list the goods used by mariners and fishermen, the following items stand out: ship boards of fir, cedars of Lebanon for masts, oars of oak, pine decking, linen for sails, iron, tin, lead, and bronze. While Ezekiel dates back to the early sixth century B.C.E., such items were still needed and available in Roman times. Tyre, Sidon, and other Mediterranean cities functioned as market centers. The residents of these cities made their livings from the sea, being traders, mariners, and fishers. "Sidon" actually means "fishery."[1]

According to scripture, Jesus visited Tyre and Sidon. There are references to the residents of those towns coming to listen to him in Galilee. Fishing trade connections between Galilee and the Mediterranean coastal cities could have provided the impetus for this link. Modern parallels abound in North America and elsewhere of the annual or semiannual buying expedition that fishermen undertake, leaving their small coastal towns and villages to journey to such centers as Seattle or Boston in the United States, St. John's in Newfoundland, or Bristol in England, where marine goods are to be found in quantity. In some parts of the world, itinerant traders selling diverse fishing supplies journey from village to village. At one time such peddlers on the Columbia River sold everything from net needles and twine to cannery equipment. In ancient times, as Willard Bascom points out in *Deep Water, Ancient Ships:* "Some ships were simply floating workshops: tinkers making and selling tools, knives, utensils; shipfitters making metal parts for ships, replacing rotted planks, selling line and spars; armorers selling weapons and protective armor."[2]

I cannot prove that Peter and his partners, including Jesus, went to the coastal cities to purchase or trade for fishing equipment, but common patterns of behavior among fishermen and scriptural references to their journeys certainly permit the possibility. In Acts 9:43 and 10:5–6, Peter stayed with Simon, a tanner in

Joppa on the Mediterranean coast. A tanner specialized in leather craft, and might reasonably be expected
to manufacture leather sails, storage skins for wine
or water, leather buckets, special leather cordage, or
other nautical items. Peter's association with Simon
could have been part of Peter's network of fishing
trade suppliers.

*Purchasing or trading for the supplies needed to
prosecute the fishing trade must have been part of
the disciples' seasonal round. Fishermen could have
obtained such articles in maritime-oriented locales like
Tyre and Sidon.*

In my mind's eye I envision Peter and his friends
taking a load of salted or smoked fish to the coast to
trade for lead, bronze needles, hemp ropes, leather
or linen sails, tanbark for dyeing web, or, alternatively,
twine or web that was already dyed.[3] All of these goods
were available on the Mediterranean coast, probably
at cheaper prices than in Galilee. In sharp contrast to
such a trading expedition, when Jesus sends out his
disciples in pairs on their healing mission (Luke 9:3;
Mark 6:8), he cautions them to take nothing for their
journey. I read this as an admonition that this not be a
trading expedition, that they are not to be sidetracked

by commerce, although they are spreading the good news through their trade networks.

Ezekiel prophesied woe to Tyre; Jesus prophesied that Tyre and Sidon would fare better in the judgment than Chorazin and Bethsaida (Matt. 11:21–22), the latter a fishing town in Galilee that rejected him. Tyre developed one of the earliest Christian communities (Acts 21:3–6). The impact of Jesus' visits and those of his fishing disciples, whether for trade or to spread the word of God's reign, is undeniable.

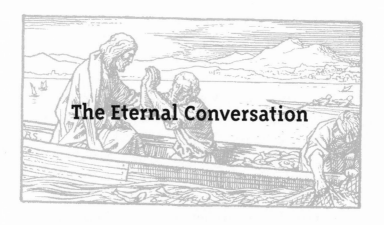

The Eternal Conversation

"And you, Capernaum, will you be exalted to heaven? No, you will be brought down to Hades. For if the deeds of power done in you had been done in Sodom, it would have remained until this day. But I tell you that on the day of judgment it will be more tolerable for the land of Sodom than for you."

—Matt. 11:23–24

I am sitting at the little table of our Southeast Alaska fishing boat, the *Blue Mist,* looking out at Pt. Baker, a remote Alaskan fishing community accessible only by water and air (weather permitting). On this hot summer Saturday, we are taking a break before a fishing period opens tomorrow. Boats are tied up everywhere in this sheltered anchorage. Someone has beached a couple of rotting hulls across the harbor in a small cove, along with a dozen rusted fifty-gallon fuel drums. The pilings in the water each have bundles of floating logs attached to them. The paraphernalia of the fishing trade is evident everywhere: buoys for the ends of nets, ropes and lines of various sizes and colors, oars and skiffs, piles of lumber, discarded web, net sheds and net racks. A radio oozes country music, a dog barks, a baby cries. Pungent smoke arises from an unseen smokehouse.

A slight riffle on the water breaks up the sun's reflection making the glittering rays dance and dazzle. And in my mind's eye, I see first-century Capernaum. Take away the country music, the oil drums, and the hum of gasoline power generators, and the real Capernaum might be surprisingly similar to this town. Perhaps there would be racks for drying fish and a bench or table for cleaning and preparing them, maybe a smokehouse or two. Undoubtedly the smell of fish would reverberate in the hot climate. Children are poking around the boats, with that age-old fascination the young have for life on the water. The boat-builder is pounding nails into a vessel under construction, while the smell of pitch from a boat being caulked prior to launching permeates the warm air. A woman comes to bring food to her husband who is busy mending his net, badly torn in the previous night's storm. Two other women are inspecting the fish drying on the racks. I eavesdrop on their conversation.

"Is it ready for market, do you think, or does it need to dry more?"

"I hear the temple in Jerusalem is looking for additional supplies of smoked fish. Zebedee had control of that market, but now that his boys have gone off with the carpenter rabbi, his catches aren't as good."

"What can you expect when all you've got is a hired crew? Not that I blame the boys for leaving. Zebedee should have retired long ago and let them have the boat. They were certainly competent to run it."

"Even the rabbi called them Boanerges, sons of thunder, they were so good at fishing in storms. And that's when the fish are moving."

"And then Zebedee's wife — trying to shove them forward so one would get to sit at the rabbi's right hand and one at his left, as if he were the Messiah! She always was pushy, but that was a bit much."

"Don't talk to me about that rabbi. I never had any use for him after he cured that Roman centurion's slave. After all we've had to put up with from the Romans, and he helps one of them! Not only that, but have you noticed that every time he goes out fishing with his buddies, they get more than the rest of us. It's not fair."

"But it's not the same around here without James and John and Simon and Andrew. I feel sorry for Simon's wife, alone so much. But at least she has her mother with her, now that the rabbi cured her."

"This community sure has changed in the last couple of years. Give that dog a kick, will you? It's after that piece of dried fish."

Competition and Cooperation

As they were coming down the mountain, Jesus ordered them, "Tell no one about the vision until after the Son of Man has been raised from the dead." — Matt. 17:9

Then Jesus ordered them to tell no one; but the more he ordered them, the more zealously they proclaimed it.

— Mark 7:36

Her parents were astounded; but he ordered them to tell no one what had happened. — Luke 8:56

He said to them, "But who do you say that I am?" Peter answered, "The Messiah of God." He sternly ordered and commanded them not to tell anyone, — Luke 9:20–21

Marine anthropologists use the term "management of information" to describe communication by fishermen.[1] "Common property resource extractors," as fishermen are classed, frequently employ secrecy regarding catch size, gear used, and locations where catches are made. Deliberate secrecy excludes the larger community that might be tempted to exploit

their fishing knowledge and hence compete with established fishers. Fishermen thus manage information
to protect themselves from competition, believing that
one person's harvest affects his neighbor's harvest,
and vice versa. Fishermen think in terms of "limited
good," meaning that there is only a limited supply of a
commodity such as fish, and that in order for one person to have more, someone else will have less. Fish
are a limited good. The person who knows how to fish
well has a competitive edge and is likely to protect
that knowledge to keep his catches high.

The fishing disciples managed information in accor-
dance with the concept of limited good, although the
Gospellers do not directly connect their practices with
fish. Recall their reaction to the person who was not of
their number but was nonetheless casting out demons
in Jesus' name (Mark 9:38–40). Jesus tells them that
"Whoever is not against us is for us." This must have
been a difficult concept for the disciples to comprehend, accustomed as they were to thinking in terms
of limited good. They were always on the cusp between cooperation and competition. Their assessment
of their position as followers of the rabbi, expressed
in terms of limited good, would be that the man casting out demons in Jesus' name was stealing part of
their catch. Further, when Jesus performed healings
but cautioned them not to tell, his admonition would
have been very understandable to them, seen as a way

of managing information so the competition did not find out about it and appropriate their evangelizing strategy. However, they would also have thought of the healings and visions as "bait" for attracting more followers, leading to a dilemma as to how to resolve two opposing viewpoints.

Fishermen think in terms of "limited good," meaning that there is only a limited supply of a commodity such as fish, and that in order for one person to have more, someone else will have less.

Wuellner makes the point that there was competition "not only between rival philosophical schools of antiquity . . . but also between rival factions or schisms in a given religion."[2] One might liken fishermen to Gnostics with secret doctrines, being "in the know." Knowledge was a limited good. Therefore they had a competitive edge over followers of other itinerant teachers, and even over other followers of Jesus, because they were in the know. However, the temptation to release information in order to swell the ranks of their leader's disciples and thus outnumber the competition must have been a constant pressure.

Jesus explained his visits to the coast to the Syro-phoenician woman (Matt. 15:24): "I was sent only to the lost sheep of the house of Israel," that is, to the Jews living in those gentile cities. His attempt to manage information about himself in these communities emerges in Mark 7:24, when he cautions his disciples not to talk about his presence in the region. We do not know his motivation. Perhaps privacy or security issues had arisen. But "he could not be hid," which is not surprising, given the ways in which such news would have spread.

Modern day anthropologists study marine gossip networks to discover how fishing communities manage and pass on information. Fishermen have the advantage of being mobile and having connections in multiple communities, through both kinship and fish buying and trading networks, so news travels rapidly. It is not hard to imagine how Jesus' reputation would have spread. On a visit to Simon the Tanner in Joppa to purchase fishing materials, Peter talks about Jesus. In the course of the next few days or weeks, Simon passes on the juicier details of miracles and healings to his other customers, who hail from other port cities. On their return to their home ports, these customers encounter other fishermen, friends, and relatives, and tell them what they have heard, perhaps embellishing the story somewhat. Their wives have a good story to tell while waiting their turn to draw water at the well or at a spinning party. Judging by the speed with which information about Jesus passed through the

Mediterranean coastal communities, so that their residents traveled many miles to hear him in Galilee, it is clear that the entire community, both Jewish and gentile, was fully aware of his reputation.

The tables are turned on the male disciples in the non-canonical Gnostic Gospel of Mary, because now it is a woman, Mary Magdalene, who has the inside track on Jesus' teaching.[3] I see elements of Gnosticism in the marine community's management of information, although Gnosticism was by no means confined to such communities. The creative tension for a faithful follower arose in managing information about Jesus. Keeping a secret makes good business sense as a fishing strategy, but denies the truth of who Jesus is, the one who makes God accessible, knowable. The fishing faithful veer between Gnosticism and openness, competition and cooperation.

The Fishermen's Pentecost

Immediately he made the disciples get into the boat and go on ahead to the other side, while he dismissed the crowds. And after he had dismissed the crowds, he went up the mountain by himself to pray. When evening came, he was there alone, but by this time the boat, battered by the waves, was far from the land, for the wind was against them. And early in the morning he came walking toward them on the sea. But when the disciples saw him walking on the sea, they were terrified, saying, "It is a ghost!" And they cried out in fear. But immediately Jesus spoke to them and said, "Take heart, it is I; do not be afraid." Peter answered him, "Lord, if it is you, command me to come to you on the water." He said, "Come." So Peter got out of the boat, started walking on the water, and came toward Jesus. But when he noticed the strong wind, he became frightened, and beginning to sink, he cried out, "Lord, save me!" Jesus immediately reached out his hand and caught him, saying

153

to him, "You of little faith, why did you doubt?" When they got into the boat, the wind ceased. And those in the boat worshiped him, saying, "Truly you are the Son of God."

— Matt. 14:22–33

On that day, when evening had come, he said to them, "Let us go across to the other side." And leaving the crowd behind, they took him with them in the boat, just as he was. Other boats were with him. A great windstorm arose, and the waves beat into the boat, so that the boat was already being swamped. But he was in the stern, asleep on the cushion; and they woke him up and said to him, "Teacher, do you not care that we are perishing?" He woke up and rebuked the wind, and said to the sea, "Peace! Be still!" Then the wind ceased, and there was a dead calm. He said to them, "Why are you afraid? Have you still no faith?" And they were filled with great awe and said to one another, "Who then is this, that even the wind and the sea obey him?"

— Mark 4:35 – 41; see also Matt. 8:23 –27 and Luke 8:22–25

Immediately he made his disciples get into the boat and go on ahead to the other side, to Bethsaida, while he dismissed the crowd. After saying farewell to them, he went up on the mountain to pray. When evening came, the boat was out on the sea, and he was alone on the land. When he saw that they were straining at the oars against an adverse wind, he came towards them early in the morning, walking on the sea. He intended to pass them by. But when they saw him walking on the sea, they thought it was a ghost and cried out; for they all saw him and were terrified. But immediately he spoke to them and said, "Take heart, it is I; do not be afraid." Then he got into the boat with them and the wind ceased. And they were utterly astounded.

— Mark 6:45–51

When evening came, his disciples went down to the sea, got into a boat, and started across the sea to Capernaum. It was now dark, and Jesus had not yet come to them. The sea became rough because a strong wind was blowing. When they had rowed about three or four miles, they saw Jesus walking on the sea and coming near the boat, and they were terrified. But he said to them, "It is I; do not be afraid." Then they wanted to take him into the boat, and immediately the boat reached the land toward which they were going.

The next day the crowd that had stayed on the other side of the sea saw that there had been only one boat there. They also saw that Jesus had not got into the boat with his disciples, but that his disciples had gone away alone. Then some boats from Tiberias came near the place where they had eaten the bread after the Lord had given thanks. So when the crowd saw that neither Jesus nor his disciples were there, they themselves got into the boats and went to Capernaum looking for Jesus. — John 6:16–24

All four Gospels contain stories of Jesus calming storms and walking on water. All four differ in details, such as destinations, or in dramatic impact. One fishing detail is contained in Mark 4, where Jesus is asleep "on the cushion." Wachsmann points out that boats carried an item called a ballast cushion.[1] This piece of information transforms the story's meaning, as the disciple's comments regarding Jesus caring nothing if they perish could have meant that they were exasperated with him for sleeping on the ballast cushion when they needed it for a sea anchor. A common way of riding out a storm is to use some form of drag to reduce the pitching of the boat. We used to lay out our net as a sea anchor in storms in Bristol Bay. John's Gospel is the most matter-of-fact and contains no claims regarding Peter's attempt to walk on water. For me, John's Gospel is most typical of the way fishermen think, as they do not tend to dwell upon danger or discuss it much. It is simply part of life. John's story concentrates instead on how Jesus got to the other side of the lake, which would be of more interest to marine people than the storm. Despite the fabulous nature of several of these Gospel passages about this incident, they are the only marine-related stories to appear in all four Gospels. Thus they deserve serious attention, despite our reluctance to deal with what appears to be the impossible.

I think there are multiple ways to approach these stories, ways that do not necessarily explain them but which allow us to treat them with respect. While our

rational, scientific, and skeptical minds are the product of our era, Peter also expressed skepticism about
water's physical ability to hold up a human being. He
set up a test. "Lord, if it is you, command me to come
to you on the water" (Matt. 14:28). It is another fisherman's version of the Doubting Thomas story. Thomas
was also a fisherman or carpenter or both, depending
upon the source consulted. Both Peter and Thomas
agree: they won't believe something unless they have
an experience. Thomas asked to see nail holes, natural enough for a carpenter. He understood nail holes.
Peter asked to walk on water. He understood water.
However, once Peter set up the test, he then had to
follow through. And of all the people in the boat, only
Peter stepped over the side.

While the story is ostensibly a pre-resurrection one,
for me it has a post-resurrection quality. The fishermen
were frightened at the appearance of Jesus "as if they
had seen a spirit." One might naturally conclude that
he was dead, if they thought they were seeing his ghost
or spirit. I think of the apparition as a natural phenomenon, the light of St. Elmo's fire. I cannot prove that it
was, but I cannot ignore the possibility either.

Another possibility reflects recent research into
near death experiences or experiences of extreme soli-
tude, such as those encountered by lone survivors of
shipwrecks. To quote Raymond Moody: "Shipwrecked
sailors stranded alone in small boats for many weeks

have described hallucinations of being rescued, sometimes by paranormal beings almost like ghosts or spirits.... In addition, many who have been isolated by shipwreck or other such events say that after a few weeks of being in this condition, they came back to civilization with a profound change of values.... Clearly, this reintegration of personality is similar to that claimed by many who have come back from death."[2]

Despite the fabulous nature of several of these Gospel passages about this incident, they are the only marine-related stories to appear in all four Gospels. Thus they deserve serious attention, despite our reluctance to deal with what appears to be the impossible.

Fishing literature is full of stories of people who have survived near-death experiences lasting only a brief period or weeks, and who had hallucinations. Later, after rescue, changes in personality arose. It is not difficult to draw parallels between such experiences with what occurred to the fishermen in the biblical storm passages.

Clearly these passages are rich with baptismal symbolism, but I think that dealing with them symbolically is not sufficient. There must have been one or more experiences with Jesus in a storm that were absolutely pivotal for the disciples. They credited him with saving their lives. Sudden violent storms arise on the Sea of Galilee due to the surrounding area's topography. The storms would feature in any fisherman's experience of the lake. I note that in Matthew (8:24) a different Greek word for storm is used than in the other Gospels, and this word can mean earthquake. The same word is found in the synoptic Gospels in connection with Jesus' death.[3] While the literary effect in Matthew is one of foreshadowing the coming of the kingdom of God, there may be another explanation for this usage. Earthquakes were fairly common in Palestine, due to its geological features, and could cause tsunamis, large waves on water. The incident Matthew describes in chapter 8 may have been such a tsunami caused by an earthquake. Whatever the cause, storms caused terror to the small-boat fishermen of Galilee.

A fisherman I know once summed up his life's experiences by saying, "Fishing is memory."[4] Certain tides, winds, and phases of the moon that once coincided to produce a good catch lead to the conclusion that the fish should be in the same place when such conditions repeat themselves. The skill lies in committing all the variables to memory and then being able to recall those memories under similar conditions. I think of the storm tales in the Bible as a mnemonic device, one that echoes scripture passages such as Psalm 107, the safe crossing of the Hebrew slaves through the Red

Sea during the Exodus, Jonah and the whale, or Noah and the Flood. The stories also remind us of Pentecost, when the great wind of the Holy Spirit came upon the disciples. I think of these accounts as the fishermen's Pentecost, though whether their experiences came before or after the event we now think of as Pentecost is not possible to say.

Whatever the underlying original incident may have been, its repetition throughout the four Gospels represents a crucial part of the oral history of the fishing community of the Sea of Galilee of that time. The stories call up important cultural memories centered on salvation and God's presence. In the story of the Exodus, the details of the forty-year journey, of who camped where and who did what are less important than the overriding meaning of the liberation of the Hebrew slaves from bondage in the land of Egypt. The Gospellers repeated the storm stories to reinforce the overarching conclusion that Jesus was God and able to save people from storms, and, by extension, all other vicissitudes of life.

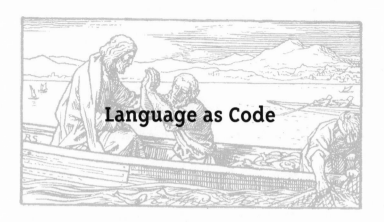

Language as Code

He became hungry and wanted something to eat; and while it was being prepared, he fell into a trance. He saw the heaven opened and something like a large sheet coming down, being lowered to the ground by its four corners. In it were all kinds of four-footed creatures and reptiles and birds of the air. Then he heard a voice saying, "Get up, Peter; kill and eat." But Peter said, "By no means, Lord; for I have never eaten anything that is profane or unclean." The voice said to him again, a second time, "What God has made clean, you must not call profane." This happened three times, and the thing was suddenly taken up to heaven.   — Acts 10:10–16

A dull overcast evening on our Southeast Alaska fish boat, the *Blue Mist.* Our net has been drifting for two hours, with very few splashes to indicate any fish in it. I am finishing washing the dishes and overhear my husband say to a friend on the radio, "It doesn't look too prosperous. I think I'm going to drag the rag and go drop the hook."

Did fishermen use the term millstone colloquially to mean anchor? It would make more sense to use a nautical term with fishermen than an agrarian term.

"Drag the rag." "Drop the hook." All around me when I am fishing I hear aphorisms, metaphors, colloquialisms, that refer to parts of the fishing operation. A fisherman planning to pull the net into the boat may say he is going to drag the rag. To drop the hook means to anchor the boat. A fisherman who uses a gillnet to catch herring might be called a "herring choker." In thinking about some of the biblical passages that have mystified me, it occurs to me that such customs may have been prevalent in the Galilean fishery too.

When I read about Jesus telling his disciples that it would be better for a millstone to be tied around a person's neck and that person be drowned in the sea (Matt. 18:6; Mark 9:42; Luke 17:2), I wonder whether he really meant a millstone. The Greek word refers to the upper grinding stone, the one with a hole in it, that somewhat resembles the stone anchors with a hole pecked in them that surface in archaeological exploration in Galilee. Did fishermen use the term millstone colloquially to mean anchor? It would make more sense to use a nautical term with fishermen than an agrarian term.

The phrase "easier for a camel to go through the eye of a needle" (Matt. 19:24; Mark 10:25; Luke 18:25) has its fishing association, as fishermen use needles to mend nets and sails. In addition, both Joachim Jeremias and Albert Nolan point out that another possible reading for camel is ship's cable or rope, which would certainly be appropriate to the fishing milieu.[1] "It is easier for your bowline to go through the eye of your sail-mending needle than for a rich man to get into heaven," translates the phrase in nautical terms. The frustration we all feel when trying to push too thick a piece of thread through the eye of a needle becomes apparent when the odd image of the camel is dropped. I had considered Jesus' pronouncement judgmental. I had not sensed Jesus' frustration in this passage until I thought of it in seamen's terms.

In Acts 10:11–12 Peter dreams of something descending from heaven "like a large sheet," with all kinds of animals, reptiles, and birds in it that God authorized for food. I wonder whether he really meant a sheet or large piece of cloth. Could it not be a colloquialism for a net, just as the fishermen of my acquaintance use the term rag? Such a meaning would be more appropriate for a fisherman's vision. Further, Peter was used to taking fish and other creatures out of a net and sorting them into clean and unclean categories. His vision becomes more powerful if it is linked with his fishing practices, as it suggests a complete reversal of what he has done all his life. Metaphorically, too, seeing a net rather than a bedsheet full of food to eat, in which clean does not have to be separated from unclean, makes more sense. The culmination of the story occurs when Peter goes to the centurion's home in Caesarea and realizes he is fishing for gentiles as well as Jews. "I truly understand that God shows no partiality, but in every nation anyone who fears him and does what is right is acceptable to him" (Acts 10:34–35). Peter sees a vision of all humanity caught up in God's net.

Spotting God

"Speak to the earth, and it shall teach thee, and the fishes of the sea shall declare unto thee."   — Job 12:8 KJV

Sunday morning on the fishing vessel *Blue Mist.* We follow a seasonal round of fishing for salmon on the Columbia River, Bristol Bay, and in Southeast Alaska, and are now in Southeast, having left Wrangell Harbor two hours ago. Breakfast is over. My husband, Kent, is topside, steering us west, toward Prince of Wales Island. I am seated at our little table, watching the ever-changing view of mountains and water. We are near St. John, opposite the Wrangell Narrows. I have been writing letters and making notes for this book. The oil stove is puttling away. Although today is Sunday, fishing season opens at noon, so I will not get to church. Instead, I have been reflecting on God, on the past, and on the scene around me, full of the paradox of the fishing life, the life that Jesus and his disciples knew intimately.

The water world around me expresses abundance and bounty, with evidence both plentiful and obvious.

But in our fishing lives we learn that God can also be subtle. We see him by signs, guessing where he may be found, just as we do the salmon. Clusters of birds in a particular spot may indicate the presence of bait, which in turn will attract the salmon. The wind direction may blow the fish closer to the beach. A flat calm is not good for fishing since fish can see the web of the net. A day with some chop on the water is best, because the shadows confuse the fish. By inference, we know where the fish may be.

By inference, too, we may try to spot God. The Galilean fishermen observed Jesus teach, heal, and speak in ways entirely different from those around him, and by inference knew that divinity was present. Jesus himself urged inference as a method of learning in Luke 12:54, using the signs of the weather to encourage them to look more deeply into the events of their day.

Once the disciples realized that God was present, it became impossible to hide their discovery. As part of the fishing community, which operates by word of mouth, I can testify how readily information spreads in this manner, even when secrecy is desirable. Fishermen devise codes to call their friends on the radio and let them know when there are fish in the vicinity. I remember sitting and listening to a radio group talking and realizing their code was about food. "Say, why don't you come over and have some blueberry pie?"

meant "I'm getting fish over here, better come quickly." Or groups will maintain silence, also a clue that something is going on. Invariably, however, a member of the group leaks some information, perhaps to a friend over a cup of coffee, or to a relative who is not part of the group and is having poor catches. Eventually the secret is out.

The fishermen learned their roles as Jesus' disciples as they would have learned a new fishing area or method, by experience. Gunnar Hermanson, an old-time Columbia River fisherman, once said, "You cannot teach anyone gillnetting. You have to do that by experience.... Every drift and tide coincides with the fishing.... You have to know each drift ... if you're interested enough, by observing, paying attention ... you can learn it by yourself."[1] After the disciples had accompanied Jesus on his travels for a while, he sent them out two by two, just as they fished in partnership on the boat, to fish for men.

I recall being anchored one calm evening in Buster Bay, watching a whale spout about a mile away. After she stopped surfacing for a while, I went below, assuming that she was around the point and out of sight. At that moment an enormous blast of air and vapor erupted ten feet off the stern of our boat. The whale had surfaced in an explosion of noise and spray. We clung to the boat, watching the huge body glide by like a submarine. Then the flukes came up as the animal sounded, and we did not see her again. We infer that God is like this, seemingly far away where you think you have left him, and then suddenly surfacing right next to you. We were not looking for such terror and such wonder so close. "The fear of the Lord is the beginning of wisdom," says the psalmist (111:10). And *ruach,* the breath or spirit of God, is not necessarily a gentle breeze. The description of the appearance of the spirit of God at Pentecost (Acts 2:2) likens it to a "mighty wind." I think back to the fishermen struggling against the storm, and wonder whether those experiences were their Pentecost, or whether Pentecost itself reflected those experiences back to them.

Jewish understanding linked fish, humans, and the Sabbath in threefold blessing. Further, they deemed the Sabbath to be the anticipation of the messianic era, "which will be inaugurated by the eating of the legendary fish Leviathan."[2] Did Jesus' post-resurrection breakfast on the beach or his appearance when he asked for a piece of broiled fish (Luke 24:42–43) signify the beginning of the great banquet for his followers? Scripture and myth contain colliding images of the future: Jonah swallowed and regurgitated by the whale; Messiah, who will capture the whale for the great feast; and Jesus, who carried out his mission with fishermen.

The Other Side of Terror

Immediately he made the disciples get into the boat and go on ahead to the other side, while he dismissed the crowds. And after he had dismissed the crowds, he went up the mountain by himself to pray. When evening came, he was there alone, but by this time the boat, battered by the waves, was far from the land, for the wind was against them. And early in the morning he came walking toward them on the sea. But when the disciples saw him walking on the sea, they were terrified, saying, "It is a ghost!" And they cried out in fear. But immediately Jesus spoke to them and said, "Take heart, it is I; do not be afraid."

Peter answered him, "Lord, if it is you, command me to come to you on the water." He said, "Come." So Peter got out of the boat, started walking on the water, and came toward Jesus. But when he noticed the strong wind, he became frightened, and beginning to sink, he cried out, "Lord, save me!" Jesus immediately reached out his hand and caught

169

him, saying to him, "You of little faith, why did you doubt?" When they got into the boat, the wind ceased. And those in the boat worshiped him, saying, "Truly you are the Son of God." — Matt. 14:22–33

What is it about my fishing life that convinces me that the biblical story is true, and of great importance? It comes down to water. For a fisher, water is an impenetrable medium, a mystery. You cannot predict failure or success on the water until you start fishing. Our skin is the shell separating us from the moisture around us, which manifests itself in a myriad of ways: as fog, mist, rain; as waves whipped to foam by the wind; as waterspouts, tornadoes composed of circulating wind and water; as ice that freezes on every plane and exposed area of the boat. Surfaces on a boat are slippery; climbing in and out of vessels subjects us to curves and shapes not found on land, rough textures, low ceilings, and the sudden swinging of a boom that makes us duck. Boots and raingear add weight to our bodies and stiffness to our movements. Lying in my bunk at night, I hear the water slap against the hull, gurgling and trickling past at the change of tide. What is under the water's surface can be known only by inference, from experience. To find out what is there by experience, demands that we be willing to risk drowning.

I struggled with the story of Jesus walking on water until a harrowing day in 1996. We were in southeast

Alaska. During the night a swell arose. We left Mary-field, our anchorage, at 3:30 a.m. in pitch blackness. While my husband went up on the flying bridge to steer, I was below, watching the depth meter drop from 52 to 22 feet of water below us in a matter of seconds. We narrowly avoided piling up on the rocks. Drift and logs were floating by; one hit could have punched a hole in the bottom of the boat. We laid out the net near the beach. We set there for an hour and half as day-light grew to the point where we could watch a whale feeding. The boat was pitching and tossing, but Kent finally got the net picked up and we went in to Mary-field to deliver the fish. We then started for Wrangell, a port town six hours away.

What is it about my fishing life that convinces me that the biblical story is true, and of great importance?

We ran the boat to the upper end of Buster Bay, which was very rough, and continued on for a couple of hours to Red Bay where we anchored to assess the situation at Snow Pass. Although Red Bay was calm, the flood tide made it hard to hold the anchor, and when we reset the anchor, we had trouble with the boat engine's starter. As it was calm in front of Red Bay, we decided to attempt to cross nearby Snow Pass in order to get the starter fixed in Wrangell. But once we passed the Eye Opener, a rocky pinnacle marked by a light, the swells grew larger and larger. To me the waves seemed to be smiling with terrible teeth, but I was managing my fear until one caught us broadside and rolled the boat. Suddenly I was high up in the air, looking straight down into green water on the other side of the boat. Kent spun the wheel to right the boat. I pitched off my seat, and four drawers and the refrigerator flew open amidst a rain of utensils, clothes, eggs and other items. With difficulty Kent turned the boat around and we headed for safety.

Walking on water? This experience showed me what terror is. I thought I knew what it was, but my earlier feelings were simply anxiety, fear, fright, not terror. Terror is a dry, cottony mouth, heaving stomach, rubbery legs, involuntary trembling, teeth chattering, and a mind completely paralyzed, incapable of doing anything except to say "Get me out of here." Think of Peter and the disciples in their boat, rowing in a storm for hours, making little headway, exhausted, unable to turn back for fear of swamping the boat. They were undoubtedly already terrorized when they saw the apparition, which I tend to think of as a natural phenomenon, such as St. Elmo's fire. In some fishing cultures, St. Elmo's fire is considered a sign of death, but it may also be a sign of good luck, particularly the end of a storm. By this time Peter is willing to do anything to be saved from the storm. A mind under such strain does not necessarily think rationally, and so he steps out of the boat in order to walk on the water to safety. However, once he gets out of the boat the storm and his terror reassert themselves, and Jesus helps him back into the boat.

The text indicates that the disciples did not recognize the apparition or spirit as Jesus until he spoke. There are many stories in the Gospels of people who did not recognize Jesus after the resurrection until he spoke, which hints that this story may be a post-resurrection one. One common interpretation is that the boat represents the early church, and without Jesus it would sink. However, I note that Peter was the only one of the disciples who stepped out of the boat. Was this a subtle message that he was the leader of the disciples, and of the early Christian church, rather than other claimants for the position?

I once saw a caption for a travel ad for Israel that invited the visitor to "Walk in the Footsteps of Jesus, with Possibly one Exception." The words were superimposed on a glorious photo of a sunset over the Sea of Galilee. The tongue-in-cheek attitude to walking on water is amusing because we do not expect to be able to do it ourselves. Can I explain how Jesus did it? No. But I can transform the experience so that it takes on meaning for me. Or I can allow the experience to transform me.

Scruffy little fishing towns exist in our time as they did in Jesus' era. The Herods are here too. But all around is the created universe that fills us with wonder. My husband and I often fish at night, so the fish will not see the net. Fish move on the change of light at dawn and dusk, and on the change of tides. They follow their watery paths through the centuries. I have stood on the flying bridge of the *Blue Mist* watching young salmon passing safely through the meshes of the net as they head out to sea at the beginning of their migration. I know that on their way home as much larger adults they will be caught by the same net. And sometimes that Zen moment comes, when I perceive the trembling of the atoms of the universe in sea fire and northern lights, in salmon scales and the sand on a vacant shore. And all becomes sacred space.

The End of Time
in Shades of Silver

Then the angel showed me the river of the water of life, bright as crystal, flowing from the throne of God....

—Rev. 22:1

We are steering through the fog to the fishing grounds in Sumner Strait, in Southeast Alaska. Our boat is not much larger than those used in Galilee so long ago, but it is infinitely more complex, with its diesel engine and multiplicity of electronic equipment. Despite our modern instruments that enable us to navigate by Global Positioning Satellite, it is easy to become confused in the fog. We are used to the sand shores and mud flats of the Columbia River, Willapa Bay, and Bristol Bay, though the Columbia has some rocky reaches. But they are familiar; they are home. On the Columbia we sometimes pass a needle of rock that juts straight up, known as Pillar Rock. In Southeast Alaska, all is rock, "unforgiving rock," as Kent puts it. Where Snow Passage and Sumner Strait meet in Southeast Alaska there is a dangerous rocky pinnacle known as the "Eye

Opener." Whales often frequent it due to the bountiful feed available there.

Fog makes us uneasy. We strain to see outside, but can discern nothing. Radio chatter from other fishermen tells of their frustration too. We reach our moorage, a shore that in the dimness looks like any other shore, but which the GPS plotter tells us is where we want to be. The anchor clanks and rattles its way to the bottom. We set a crab trap, hoping for crab for dinner. The fog eventually lifts, and we are indeed where we wanted to be. Small seabirds pick at food among the kelp beds. An otter is lolloping along the rocky shore. A salmon jumps three, no four, times. "Humpy," grumbles one of our companions, referring to the small pink fleshed salmon that has the least monetary value. We are rafted alongside two other boats. I can never identify what kinds of salmon are jumping. It always amazes me when someone can do it from such a distance. But then, I can't tell cars apart either.

We decide to share our supper of crab, bread, salad, and huckleberry pie with the others, who in turn bring their offerings. There is lots of laughter as we climb from boat to boat, sharing the cramped quarters, limited cutlery, and even more limited wine glasses. I remember reading that a cooking pot was found nestled near the first-century boat excavated from the mud of the Sea of Galilee, which precipitated a scholarly discussion about the meaning of its location and its possible uses. Let the academics argue; I know why it was there. I hope those long ago forebears enjoyed their shared meal. A Columbia River gillnetter once reminisced about his years fishing and the meals he had shared with others. "It was a celebration, the fishing was a celebration."[1]

I remember my husband and a fundamentalist friend of ours talking about the Apocalypse once. While agreeing on little else, they did agree on one thing: "It will be an ecological collapse." The end of time in shades of silver.

About a mile away a solitary boat is anchored, holding a show. The boat's owner is warning other fishermen that this is the place he has marked out to set his net when the season opens twenty-four hours from now. The others joke about his dog-eat-dog style. Since there is not a lot of fish around, such behavior is a little more competitive than circumstances warrant. I think that James and John must have been like this, trying to hold a show for themselves in the places closest to Jesus in his coming kingdom, and being viewed by the others as overly aggressive.

Occasionally one of us responds to a radio call from someone still on their way to the fishing grounds.

"How's the weather down there?"

"Clear, now the fog's lifted. What about where you are?"

"Still foggy. Can't see my hat."

"Are you going to cross over tonight or wait at St. John?"

"I think I'll keep coming. At least the water's flat calm."

A line comes to me from Psalm 121: "The Lord shall preserve thy going out and thy coming in." Yet all of us know that not everyone comes home safely. We have all been out in dirty weather, have all taken our chances that our boat will float, that a wave will not swamp us, that we will not hit a rock, that our engine will not die. We have all been out in our rain-gear pulling in the net when green water washes over the stern, swirling around our boots and sluicing out through the scuppers. We have all tried to keep our footing when the wind bobs the boat around, knocking cold salt spray in our eyes, and the jellyfish are hanging in gobs from the net, ready to sting any exposed flesh. We all know someone who has died at sea. But Kent and I are witnessing the death of the salmon runs of the Columbia, and it brings a larger grief, a wound that will not heal.

Hobe Kytr wrote a poem as a memorial for the fishermen who have lost their lives on the Columbia.

Drifting in the dark at the edge of the world,
At one with the work while others sleep,
As all around the waters swirled,
Soft sifts the net through the moonlit deep
Of a freshet of fish
With a prayerful wish
To seek the shoals of salmon.

Mother of rivers! Your rhythm runs in my blood.
But whither beckons this seductive urge
To taste the one true water on the flood?
Is fate but to follow this pulsing surge?
Yet fresh, like the fish,
An undying wish,
To seek the shoals of salmon.[2]

The shoals of Columbia River salmon are a shadow of their former abundance and are still in decline, unable to compromise with civilization in all its forms that needs water for irrigation, power, dredged shipping lanes, and sewage disposal. My husband and I have come from our home in the lower Columbia's rain forest deeper into the rain forest in Alaska, and for a brief period each year that death on the Columbia is left behind. I remember my husband and a fundamentalist friend of ours talking about the Apocalypse once. While agreeing on little else, they did agree on one thing: "It will be an ecological collapse." The end of time in shades of silver.

In the predawn the fog is back. We pull up the anchor and head out for the nearby fishing ground, to lay out the net once again and be surprised once again at what it brings to us. As we glide through a blind world on black and deep water, we turn to each other and then look at the crucifix hanging on the wall. Water and death. Rock and death. Fish and death.

Water of baptism. Rock of salvation. ICHTHUS.

Glossary

Amphlibestron. *See* Cast net.

Anchorage. A sheltered place with a bottom configuration suitable for anchoring a boat.

Buoy. A marker for the end of a net.

Cast net (Gk. *amphlibestron*). A portable circular net thrown by a fisherman from shore or from a boat. As it is thrown, it opens like an umbrella, then sinks to the bottom of the water, trapping fish under it. Fish are removed by pulling them through the meshes.

Caulk. To render a boat watertight by applying a substance such as pitch to the seams between the planks.

Cork. *See* Float.

Diktyon, Diktya. *See* Gillnet.

Diver. On the Columbia River, a net that is fished on the ebb tide.

Drift. To ply a river or body of water with a net, on either the flood or the ebb tide. Also, on the Columbia River, a section of river bottom from which the snags and other obstructions have been removed. The organization of those who fish a given drift area.

Drift right. An individual fisherman's share or membership in a drift.

Fathom. A standard measure of six feet.

Float. A device used on the corkline of a net to provide buoyancy; also called a cork.

Floater. On the Columbia River, a net that is fished mainly on the flood tide and slack water.

Flying Bridge. The upper uncovered deck of a boat.

Gaff. A large metal hook on a handle, used to pull a fish on board.

Gillnet (Gk. *diktyon, diktya*). A net that has floats attached to the top line (corkline) and weights to the bottom line (leadline) so it will hang perpendicularly in the water. Fish swim into the net, become entangled in its meshes, and are removed from the net when it is pulled from the water. Also a verb, to fish with a gillnet.

Grapple. A large hook with several prongs, tied to a rope, used to drag along the bottom of a body of water to retrieve submerged items. Also known as a grapple hook or grapple iron.

Hang. To sew web onto a corkline or leadline.

Highliner. A fisherman whose catches are consistently above average.

Hold a show. *See* Show.

Hook-and-line. A means of fishing with a baited hook that attracts fish.

Killick. A handmade stone anchor.

Knit. To create web from twine.

Lay out. To set out a net in the water.

Lead. Molded piece of lead attached to the bottom line of a gillnet or seine.

Leadline. A weighted line used on the bottom edge of a gillnet or seine.

Mesh. The diamond shaped portion of the web of the gillnet.

Needle. A wooden or plastic device filled with twine, used for mending, sewing, or hanging a net.

Net rack. A structure with rails over which nets are pulled to dry or for mending.

Pick. To pull the net into the boat after a drift is made. Also, to take the fish out of the net.

Rack. To spread a net to dry over rails in a net rack.

Reel. A large spool in a boat, on which the net is wound.

Sagene. *See* Seine.

Saint Elmo's Fire. A static electrical charge that appears on masts, steeples and high places during an electrical storm.

Seine (Gk. *sagene*). A net with heavy meshes designed to be laid out to surround a school of fish, which can then be pulled in to shore and the fish removed.

Sew. To attach two pieces of web together.

Show. The distance between two boats fishing simultaneously. The more distance between the two, the better the chance of making a good haul. To hold a show is to anchor on the spot where the net will be laid out, thus warning other fishermen to keep their distance.

Snag. A log or other obstruction on the bottom of a body of water. Also, to tear one's gear on an obstruction.

Towhead. The place where fishermen of a given drift right wait their turn to lay out their nets.

Trammel Net. A wall of large mesh, hung on one or both sides of a wall of smaller-meshed gear, designed so a fish striking the smaller mesh net pushes it through to form a pocket in which it becomes trapped.

Trap. A form of stationary fish gear with an entrance that fish swim into, and then cannot exit.

Web. The net portion of a gillnet or seine.

Research Methods

This book has been with me a long time, although I wrote it in a relatively short period. I have spent close to thirty years fishing on the Columbia River, on Willapa Bay, and in Alaska with my husband, Kent, on our three boats, the *Floozie,* the *Blue Mist,* and the *Dorleen.* I have spent over twenty of those years devoted to the study of fishing cultures and completing the research for this book. However, the text is as much the result of serendipity as it is of formal research. I have done formal literature surveys, but I have also found that as I talked with people, questioned them, and wrote letters to sources, certain pieces of information have come my way that I never could have found through literature surveys alone. I have been methodical, I hope, but I must admit that madness has crept in too!

I have interwoven history with observations of present-day fishing, both from my own experience and that of others, and with my reflections on my own experiences. I could have written a book simply on the academic material available about Jesus' fishing followers, but it would have been false to have pretended that this information has had no impact on my life or faith. I believe that scientific study is seldom value neutral. Each writer has a unique personal background that must influence the content of scholarship, no matter how hard we try to keep our prejudices at bay or disguise our predilections. I would rather be honest and state that I have been influenced by being part of the fishing world, and that this influence may be viewed both as a strength and a weakness. Those looking for insight into the fishing world of the Mediterranean of the first century can be assured that that is what I too was searching for.

We are very fortunate to live in a period of great insight and scholarly study of the Bible which I believe has brought us closer to understanding the Mediterranean culture of the time of Christ. The sheer wealth of information and richness of thought available to students of the Bible in our era has provided me with many hours of delightful reading. I have made a point of quoting reputable and popular sources such as recent Bible dictionaries, *National Geographic,* and the *Biblical Archaeology Review* as a guide to readers who wish to pursue a topic further. Usually these articles derive from the latest scholarly and scientific work in the fields, but they have the advantage of being readable and accessible. Much scholarly publishing is inaccessible except to those in large cities with major theological libraries or to those who have access to a sophisticated interlibrary loan network, as the work is frequently published in obscure journals or by foreign publishers with tenuous marketing connections in North America. The Internet lends itself to exploration of obscure topics and new scientific discoveries.

The discipline of marine anthropology indicates that some features of maritime cultures are common worldwide. Additionally, the Galilee fisheries survived relatively unchanged into the twentieth century, still in living memory. Some material exists regarding their technology and those of other current, small-craft artisanal fisheries. I believe that today's fishing communities and their cultures contain much that parallels the fishing communities of the Bible. I have used my own experiences and those of other fishers where they seemed to illustrate a point made in the Bible and clarify what may have been happening. However, there is undoubtedly much that I have missed. Some things I have found baffling. I may simply be mistaken on some issues. I accept responsibility for my errors.

All biblical quotations are taken from the New Revised Standard Version, unless otherwise indicated. The poem by Hobe Kytr is reprinted courtesy of the author.

Notes

The Fishing Occupation (pp. 11–17)

1. "Skamokawa Pete" Peterson, personal communication regarding the custom of anchoring the bottom edge of fish traps with stones on the Columbia River.

2. Mendel Nun, *The Sea of Galilee and Its Fishermen in the New Testament* (Kibbutz Ein Gev, Israel: Tourist Department and Kinnereth Sailing Co., 1989), 20.

3. Cecil Moberg, personal communication.

The Invisible Works of the Lord (pp. 18–25)

1. Northrop Frye, *The Great Code* (Toronto: Academic Press Canada, 1982).

2. The following *National Geographic* articles were consulted: "Geographical Twins a World Apart," 114, no. 6 (December 1958): 858; Kenneth MacLeish, "The Land of Galilee," 128, no. 6 (December 1965): 858–59; Howard La Fay, "Where Jesus Walked," 132, no. 6 (December 1967): 760; Harvey Arden, "The Living Dead Sea," 153, no. 2 (February 1978): 224–45; Don Belt, "Living in the Shadow of Peace — Israel's Galilee," 187, no. 6 (June 1995): 62–87. See also "Fishermen Face a New Era on the Sea of Galilee," *The Fish Boat* (April 1987): 29.

3. Joseph Zias, "Anthropological Observations," in *The Excavations of an Ancient Boat in the Sea of Galilee (Lake Kinneret),* ed. Shelley Wachsmann, Atiquot 19 (Jerusalem: Israel Antiquities Authority, 1990), 125.

4. Sarah Bittleman, *Commercial Fishers: An Endangered Species* (New York: Seamen's Church Institute of New York and New Jersey, 1980), 1.

5. Basil Harley, *Church Ships: A Handbook of Votive and Commemorative Models* (Norwich: Canterbury Press, 1994), 51–72,

describes a number of such models in the U.K. I have seen them in churches in the United States and Canada as well.

The Smell of Death and Money (pp. 26–30)

1. Interview with Bill Gunderson by Jim Bergeron, December 16, 1988, Astoria, Oregon, Columbia River Maritime Museum, 40–41.

2. Robert Michael Pyle, *The Thunder Tree: Lessons from an Urban Wildland* (Boston: Houghton Mifflin, 1993), 145.

3. John Kinch, "Love of Life," *Nature Conservancy* 46, no. 2 (March–April 1996): 8.

4. As quoted in "The Greenland Whale Fishery," *Sea Heritage News* 13 (1983): 28.

The Calling of Two Brothers (pp. 31–40)

1. I point out also the Gospel of the Ebionites and its calling story, as found in Willis Barnstone, ed., *The Other Bible* (San Francisco: HarperSanFrancisco, 1984), 337: "There appeared a certain man named Jesus of about thirty years of age, who chose us. And when he came to Capernaum, he entered into the house of Simon whose surname was Peter and opened his mouth and said: As I passed the Lake of Tiberias, I chose John and James, the sons of Zebedee, and Simon and Andrew and Thaddaeus and Simon the Zealot and Judas the Iscariot, and you, Matthew, I called as you sat at the receipt of custom, and you followed me. You, therefore, I will to be twelve apostles for a testimony unto Israel."

The book known as the Acts of John (Barnstone, *The Other Bible,* 417) also has a calling story: "For when he had chosen Peter and Andrew, who were brothers, he came to me and to my brother James, saying 'I need you; come with me!' And my brother said this to me, 'John, what does he want, this child on the shore who called us?' And I said, 'Which child?' And he answered me, 'The one who is beckoning to us.' And I said 'This is because of the long watch we have kept at sea. You are not seeing straight, brother James. Do you not see the man standing there who is handsome, fair and cheerful looking?'"

189

The book goes on to describe Jesus in a variety of appearances. Any fisherman who has waited out the long hours on watch could verify the notion that John might be fatigued. However, there are too many elements of the fabulous in this passage to justify any claim to authority.

2. It is difficult to ascertain how many disciples were fishermen. We know from the Gospels that Simon Peter and Andrew and James and John followed the trade. The final chapter of the Gospel of John lists Thomas the twin, Nathanael of Cana in Galilee, and two other disciples as getting into the boat with Peter. I doubt that non-fishing disciples would have joined in a fishing expedition after Jesus' death, and believe that the list of participants in this trip is our best evidence as to the identity of the fishermen followers. There is some conjecture that Nathanael and Bartholomew were one and the same. The other two unnamed disciples mentioned in John's Gospel could have been Andrew and Philip, which would bring the total to seven. Matthew, as will be seen, was tax collector and fish licenser, making eight connected with the occupation.

3. Barnstone, *The Other Bible,* 466.

4. M. Estellie Smith, "Comments on the Heuristic Utility of Maritime Anthropology," *Maritime Anthropologist* 1, no. 1 (Summer 1977): 2–5, 8.

5. For an in-depth discussion of egalitarianism, see John Crossan, *Jesus: A Revolutionary Biography* (San Francisco: Harper-SanFrancisco, 1994), 68–73.

6. Mendel Nun, *The Sea of Galilee and Its Fishermen in the New Testament* (Kibbutz Ein Gev, Israel: Tourist Department and Kinnereth Sailing Co., 1989), 20, 46.

7. James Mays, ed., *Harper's Bible Commentary* (San Francisco: HarperSanFrancisco, 1988), 970.

The Sons of Thunder (pp. 41–45)

1. Interview with Bill Gunderson by Jim Bergeron, December 16, 1988, Astoria, Oregon, Columbia River Maritime Museum, 37.

2. Mendel Nun, *The Sea of Galilee and Its Fishermen in the New Testament* (Kibbutz Ein Gev, Israel: Tourist Department and Kinnereth Sailing Co., 1989), 6–9.

3. "Fiddler's Green," sung by the Irish Rovers in their album *On the Shores of Americay,* MCA Records, 1971.

4. See, for example, *The Interpreter's Bible* (New York: Abingdon, 1951), 7:688.

The Three Who Followed (pp. 46–48)

1. William S. McBirnie, *The Search for the Twelve Apostles* (Wheaton, Ill.: Tyndale House, 1973), 130.

2. Ibid., 142; "The Gospel of Thomas," in *The Other Bible,* ed. Willis Barnstone (San Francisco: HarperSanFrancisco, 1984), 466.

3. John MacGregor, *The Rob Roy on the Jordan, Nile, Red Sea, & Gennesareth, &c.: A Canoe Cruise in Palestine and Egypt, and the Waters of Damascus* (London: John Murray, 1869, reprint by Long Riders' Guild Press, 2001), 328.

Marine Symbolism (pp. 49–53)

1. Northrop Frye, *The Great Code* (Toronto: Academic Press Canada, 1982), 147.

2. "On Baptism 1–9," in *Documents in Early Christian Thought,* ed. Maurice Wiles (Cambridge: Cambridge University Press, 1975), 173.

3. Rev. S. Thelwall, trans., "On Baptism," in *The Ante-Nicene Fathers,* ed. Alexander Roberts and James Donaldson (Grand Rapids, Mich.: Wm. B. Eerdmans, 1986), 3:669.

4. Heather Child and Dorothy Colles, *Christian Symbols, Ancient and Modern: A Handbook for Students* (London: G. Bell and Sons, 1971), 211, 230, 220, 15.

5. Carl Jung, *Aion: Researches into the Phenomenology of the Self,* trans. R. F. C. Hull, Bollingen Series 20 (Princeton, N.J.: Princeton University Press, 1978), 89–91.

6. Ibid., 111–13.

7. Edmund Leach, "Fishing for Men," in *The Literary Guide to the Bible,* ed. Robert Alter and Frank Kermode (Cambridge, Mass.: Belknap Press of Harvard University Press, 1987), 593–95.

The Fish of Galilee (pp. 54–57)

1. Vernon K. Robbins, "The Social Location of the Implied Author," in *The Social World of Luke/Acts,* ed. Jerome Neyrey (Peabody, Mass.: Hendrickson, 1991), 319.

2. Mendel Nun, *The Sea of Galilee and Its Fishermen in the New Testament* (Kibbutz Ein Gev, Israel: Tourist Department and Kinnereth Sailing Co., 1989), 6–11.

3. Ibid., 10.

4. Joseph Telushkin, *Jewish Literacy* (New York: William Morrow, 1991), 635.

Three Herods (pp. 58–61)

1. See, for example, Barbara Burrell, Kathryn Gleason, and Ehud Netzer, "Uncovering Herod's Seaside Palace," *Biblical Archaeology Review* 19, no. 3 (May–June 1993): 50–57, 76, and Robert Hohlfelder, "Herod the Great's City on the Sea: Caesarea Maritima," *National Geographic* 171, no. 2 (February 1987): 260–79.

2. Richard Bates, "Sepphoris: An Urban Portrait of Jesus," *Biblical Archaeology Review* 18, no. 3 (May–June 1992): 55, 62.

3. Information from John Drane, *Introducing the New Testament* (San Francisco: Harper and Row, 1986), 33–34; W. O. E. Oesterly, *A History of Israel* (Oxford: Clarendon Press, 1951), 2:388–96; D. S. Russell, *The Jews from Alexander to Herod* (London: Oxford University Press, 1967), 95–110.

4. "Life of Flavius Josephus," in *The Works of Josephus,* trans. William Whiston (Peabody, Mass.: Hendrickson, 1987), 5.

5. Josephus, *Wars of the Jews,* in ibid., book 3, chapters 9, 10.

Abundance and Scarcity (pp. 62–72)

1. Bruce Metzger and Michael Coogan, eds., *The Oxford Companion to the Bible* (New York: Oxford University Press, 1993), 242.

2. Flavius Josephus, *The Wars of the Jews,* in *The Works of Josephus,* trans. William Whiston (Peabody, Mass.: Hendrickson, 1987), book 3, chapter 10, 662.

3. *Encyclopaedia Judaica* (Jerusalem: Macmillan, 1971), 6:1327.

4. Howard C. Kee, "Sociology of the New Testament," in *Harper's Bible Dictionary,* ed. Paul Achtemeier (San Francisco: Harper-SanFrancisco, 1985), 961.

5. John Crossan, *The Birth of Christianity* (San Francisco: HarperSanFrancisco, 1998), 223.

6. Ibid., 221.

7. Jonathan Reed, "Places in Early Christianity: Galilee, Archaeology, Urbanization, and Q." Ph.D. Diss., Claremont Graduate School (Ann Arbor, Mich.: University Microfilms International, 1994), as quoted in Crossan, *The Birth of Christianity,* 221.

8. Rami Arav and Richard Freund, *Bethsaida: A City by the North Shore of the Sea of Galilee* (Kirksville, Mo.: Thomas Jefferson State University Press, 1995), 1:75.

9. Todd Van Beck, *The Cemetery History Book* (Covington, Ky.: Loewen Group, 1994), 21.

10. Shelley Wachsmann, *The Sea of Galilee Boat: An Extraordinary 2000-Year-Old Discovery* (New York: Plenum Press, 1995), 251–55.

11. W. H. Wuellner, *The Meaning of "Fishers of Men"* (Philadelphia: Westminster Press, 1967), 61.

12. O. H. Oren, "Physical and Chemical Characteristics of Lake Tiberias," *Bulletin of the Research Council of Israel* 11G, no. 1 (May 1962): 1, 9.

13. It is difficult to identify with precision environmental factors that could have had an effect on the lake. As Karl Butzer put it: "Third order [climatic] anomalies affecting smaller areas and for shorter periods of time are hinted at by modern observational data.... But current geoarchaeological observations tend to be too coarse-grained to identify them." He also points out that "in arid environments, where resources such as water and food are at a premium ... second order anomalies can be expected to have some measure of real significance, at least locally, well beyond the impact of similar oscillations in more bountiful climates" ("Environmental Change in the Near East and Human Impact on the Land," in *Civilizations of the Ancient Near East,* ed. Jack Sasson [New York: Simon and Schuster and Prentice Hall International, 1995], 1:138).

14. Arav and Freund, *Bethsaida: A City,* 1:67. See also Rami Arav, Richard Freund, and John Shroder, "Bethsaida Rediscovered," *Biblical Archaeology Review* 26, no. 1, (January–February 2000), 46, 48, 52, 56 for a discussion regarding geological processes in the region.

15. Arav and Freund, *Bethsaida: A City,* 1:70.

16. Ibid., 1:89.

17. My observations are echoed in Barbara J. Garrity-Blake's study of the fishermen of Carteret County: *To Fish or Not to Fish: Occupational Transitions within the Commercial Fishing Community of Carteret County, N.C.* (Greenville, N.C.: East Carolina University Press, 1996), 1. She found that fishermen trying to adapt to poor fishing conditions were very flexible in switching in and out of gear types and also straddled "both fishing and non-fishing sources of income." Likewise, Bonnie McCay's work with Newfoundland fishermen found a variety of adaptive mechanisms used by fishermen in coping with changes in fisheries, in "Systems Ecology, People Ecology and the Anthropology of Fishing Communities," *Human Ecology* 6, no. 4 (1978): 397–422.

The Roman Impact on the Fishing Business (pp. 73–80)

1. Douglas Edwards, "The Socio-Economic and Cultural Ethos of the Lower Galilee in the First Century: Implications for the Nascent Jesus Movement," in *The Galilee in Late Antiquity,* ed. Lee Levine (New York: Jewish Theological Seminary of America, 1992), 61.

2. Ibid., 55.

3. Carolyn Creed, "It's Not a Job, It's a Lifestyle." *Cross Currents* 2 (Autumn 1988): 85.

4. W. H. Wuellner, *The Meaning of "Fishers of Men"* (Philadelphia: Westminster Press, 1967), 61.

5. William Barclay, *The Master's Men* (New York: Abingdon: 1959), 34, is simply one source for this legend.

6. Wuellner, *The Meaning of "Fishers of Men,"* 21–25, 42–43, 61–63.

7. Jennifer Gilden and Courtland Smith, *Adapting to Change: Survey of Gillnetters in Oregon and Washington, Summary of Results* (Corvallis, Ore.: Oregon Sea Grant, 1996), 5, 6, 10.

Fishing Gear (pp. 83–87)

1. John J. Rousseau and Rami Arav, *Jesus and His World: An Archaeological and Cultural Dictionary* (Minneapolis: Fortress Press, 1995), 94.

2. Donna Olson, "Georgia Maki, Astoria Net Mender," in *North Coast Folklife Festival,* ed. Suzi Jones (Astoria: Oregon Arts Commission, 1977), 19–21.

3. Mendel Nun, *The Sea of Galilee and Its Fishermen in the New Testament* (Kibbutz Ein Gev, Israel: Tourist Department and Kinnereth Sailing Co., 1989), 16–21.

4. Eric Bishop, "Jesus and the Lake," *Catholic Biblical Quarterly* 13 (1951): 401–2.

5. Nun, *The Sea of Galilee,* 28–34.

6. Ibid., 23.

7. Alexander Walker, *An Account of a Voyage to the Northwest Coast of America in 1785 and 1786,* ed. Robin Fisher and J. Bumsted (Seattle: University of Washington Press, 1982), 112–13.

8. Nun, *The Sea of Galilee,* 30; Bishop, "Jesus and the Lake," 404.

9. I am indebted to the Rev. Robin Moore (personal communication), for pointing out these similarities.

Jesus the Fisherman (pp. 88–93)

1. See, for example, *The New American Bible for Catholics* (Iowa Falls, Iowa: World Bible Publishers, 1991), 1167, note.

2. John Spong, *Resurrection: Myth or Reality?* (San Francisco: HarperSanFrancisco, 1994), 192, makes the point that this chapter may have its origins in a very primitive tradition and therefore be older than usually thought.

3. Robert J. Miller, ed., *The Complete Gospels* (Sonoma, Calif.: Polebridge Press, 1992), 401.

4. Quoted in *Work Is Our Joy: The Story of the Columbia River Gillnetter,* video written by Irene Martin, produced by Lawrence Johnson, Oregon State University Extension Sea Grant and Columbia River Maritime Museum, 1989.

The Tax Collector (pp. 99–104)

1. W. H. Wuellner, *The Meaning of "Fishers of Men"* (Philadelphia: Westminster Press, 1967), 21.

2. Ibid., 21–25, 42–43, 61–63. See also M. Rostovtzeff, *The Social and Economic History of the Roman Empire* (Oxford: Clarendon Press, 1971), 1:297; 3:689–90.

3. William Barclay, *The Master's Men* (New York: Abingdon, 1959), 34, is one source of this notion.

4. Wuellner, *The Meaning of "Fishers of Men,"* 42–43.

5. Douglas Edwards, "The Socio-Economic and Cultural Ethos of the Lower Galilee in the First Century: Implications for the Nascent Jesus Movement," in *The Galilee in Late Antiquity,* ed. Lee Levine (New York: Jewish Theological Seminary of North America, 1992), 55.

The One Who Isn't There (pp. 105–107)

1. Bruce Metzger and Michael Coogan, eds., *The Oxford Companion to the Bible* (New York: Oxford University Press, 1993), 395.

Women in Fishing (pp. 108–113)

1. M. Estellie Smith, "Comments on the Heuristic Utility of Maritime Anthropology," *Maritime Anthropologist* 1, no. 1 (Summer 1977): 2–5, 8.

2. Examples include Fran Danowski, *Fishermen's Wives: Coping with an Extraordinary Occupation,* Marine Bulletin 37 (Narragansett: University of Rhode Island Press, 1980); Charlene Allison, Sue-Ellen Jacobs, and Mary Porter, *Winds of Change: Women in Northwest Commercial Fishing* (Seattle: University of Washington Press, 1989); Leslie Leyland Fields, *The Entangling Net: Alaska's Commercial Fishing Women Tell Their Lives* (Urbana: University of Illinois Press, 1997).

3. Interview with Jack Marincovich by Jim Bergeron, November 2, 1988, Astoria, Oregon, Columbia River Maritime Museum, 8.

4. Interview with Georgia Maki by Jim Bergeron, n.d., Astoria, Oregon, Columbia River Maritime Museum, 42.

5. Abraham Rihbany, *The Syrian Christ* (Boston: Houghton Mifflin, 1916), 358–61.

6. K. C. Hanson, "The Galilean Fishing Economy and the Jesus Tradition," *Biblical Theology Bulletin* 27, no. 3 (Fall 1997): 11–12.

7. Michah Rynor, "Market Power," *University of Toronto Magazine* (Summer 1999): 7.

8. Jack Finegan, *The Archaeology of the New Testament* (Princeton, N.J.: Princeton University Press, 1992), 107–10.

An Independent Woman (pp. 114–115)

1. Susan Haskins, *Mary Magdalen: Myth and Metaphor* (New York: Harcourt, Brace, 1993), 12–15.

2. Pat Simpson, "Church of Mary Magdalen," *Annual Source Newsletter,* Church Council of Greater Seattle (November 1998): 1.

The Seller of Purple (pp. 116–119)

1. Edith Dean, *All of the Women of the Bible* (New York: Harper, 1955), 221–26.

2. Valerie Abrahamsen, *Women and Worship at Philippi: Diana/Artemis and Other Cults in the Early Christian Era* (Portland, Me.: Astarte Shell Press, 1995), 11.

3. *World Book Encyclopedia* (Chicago: World Book, 1994), 15: 392; Maitland Edey and the eds., *The Sea Traders* (Alexandria, Va.: Time-Life Books, 1974), 61; Avner Raban and Robert Stieglitz, "The Sea Peoples and Their Contributions to Civilization," *Biblical Archaeology Review* 17, no. 6 (November–December 1991): 34–42; Ephraim Stern, "The Persistence of Phoenician Culture," *Biblical Archaeology Review* (May–June 1993): 38–49, esp. 47–49; Michael Coogan, "Canaanites: Who Were They and Where Did They Live?" *Bible Review* (June 1993): 44–45.

4. P'til Tekhelet, "Top Ten Tekhelet FAQ's and Facts," website for the Association for the Promotion and Distribution of Tekhelet, *www.tekhelet.com,* Jerusalem. See also Matthew 4:13–15, for the association of Zebulun, Naphtali, and Galilee.

5. Valerie Abrahamsen, *Women and Worship,* 23, note 34.

6. *Interpreter's Dictionary of the Bible* (New York: Abingdon, 1962), 3:192; Emil Kraeling, *Rand McNally Bible Atlas* (New York: Rand McNally, 1956), 469–70.

7. See, for example, Paul's Epistle to the Philippians, 4:2–3, which mentions Euodia and Syntyche, whose disagreement had provoked a crisis in the church, and Revelation 2:20–23, where "Jezebel" had caused a serious upset in the church at Thyatira. Valerie Abrahamsen, *Women and Worship,* describes women's roles in other cults at Philippi.

Fishing Rights (pp. 120–125)

1. See for example Kent Martin, "Play by the Rules or Don't Play at All: Space Division and Resource Allocation in a Rural Newfoundland Fishing Community," *North Atlantic Maritime Cultures,* ed. Raoul Andersen (The Hague: Mouton, 1979), 277–98; John Cordell, *A Sea of Small Boats,* Cultural Survival Report 26 (Cambridge, Mass.: Cultural Survival Inc., 1989); Christopher Dyer and James McGoodwin, eds., *Folk Management in the World's Fisheries* (Niwot: University Press of Colorado, 1994). My own work on drift rights on the Columbia River, *Legacy and Testament, the Story of Columbia River Gillnetters* (Pullman: Washington State University Press, 1994) is another example of numerous works in the area of territoriality among fishermen.

2. Theodore Panayotou, *Territorial Use Rights in Fisheries,* FAO Fish Report No. 289, Supplement (Rome: United Nations Food and Agricultural Organization, 1984), 154.

3. Martin, *Legacy and Testament,* 103.

4. George Adam Smith, *The Historical Geography of the Holy Land* (London: Hodder and Stoughton, 1897), 425–26.

5. Mendel Nun, *The Sea of Galilee and Its Fishermen in the New Testament* (Kibbutz Ein Gev, Israel: Tourist Department and Kinnereth Sailing Co., 1989), 20; Vassilios Tzaferis, *The Excavations of Kursi-Gergesa,* Atiquot 16, English Series (Jerusalem: Department of Antiquities and Museums, 1983), 41–42 [Atiquot was also published in Hebrew with different numbering].

6. Rami Arav and Richard Freund, eds., *Bethsaida: A City by the North Shore of the Sea of Galilee* (Kirksville, Mo.: Thomas Jefferson State University Press, 1995), vol. 1, and John J. Rousseau and Rami Arav, *Jesus and His World: An Archaeological and Cultural Dictionary* (Minneapolis: Fortress Press, 1995), 94.

7. *Encyclopaedia Judaica* (Jerusalem: Macmillan, 1971), 6:1326–27.

8. Nun, *The Sea of Galilee,* 24, 46.

9. Ibid., 38.

10. Ibid., 16–17.

The Thin Places (pp. 126–130)

1. Some time after writing this, I ran across Marcus Borg's view that Jesus himself was one of the thin places, in Marcus Borg and N. T. Wright, *The Meaning of Jesus: Two Visions* (San Francisco: HarperSanFrancisco, 1998), 250.

2. Keith Heidorn, "Weather Phenomenon and Elements: The Fire of St. Elmo," *The Weather Doctor, Spectrum Educational Enterprises,* website *www.islandnet.com,* May 30, 1998, and Sean Palmer, "St. Elmo's Fire," Earth Light Resource, 1999–2002, website *www.mysterylights.com.*

3. Abraham Rihbany, *The Syrian Christ* (Boston: Houghton Mifflin, 1916), 221–23.

The Hiding Place (pp. 131–135)

1. Interview with Ross Lindstrom, April 19, 1988, Astoria, Oregon, Columbia River Maritime Museum, 8.

2. Mendel Nun, *The Sea of Galilee and Its Fishermen in the New Testament* (Kibbutz Ein Gev, Israel: Tourist Department and Kinnereth Sailing Co., 1989), 59.

3. Ibid., 59.

4. Recall the parable of salt used as a preservative in Matthew 5:13. Jesus points out that if *salt* (emphasis mine) has lost its saltiness, it can no longer preserve anything. In that hot climate, salt was a valued commodity to preserve food such as fish that would otherwise spoil rapidly. For a more detailed discussion of fish preservation, see K. C. Hanson, "The Galilean Fishing Economy and the Jesus Tradition," *Biblical Theology Bulletin* 27, no. 3 (Fall 1997): 99–111.

5. Ibid., 11–12.

6. Robert J. Miller, ed., *The Complete Gospels* (Sonoma, Calif.: Polebridge Press, 1992), 306. See also Robert Funk, Roy Hoover,

and the Jesus Seminar, *The Five Gospels* (New York: Macmillan [Polebridge Press], 1993), where this same text is compared to a proverb recorded by Aesop.

7. John Rousseau and Rami Arav, *Jesus and His World: An Archaeological and Cultural Dictionary* (Minneapolis: Fortress Press, 1995), 121.

The Boats of Galilee (pp. 136–139)

1. Information about the Galilee boat is summarized from Shelley Wachsmann's article "The Galilee Boat: 2000-Year-Old Hull Recovered Intact," *Biblical Archaeology Review* 14, no. 5 (September–October 1988): 18–33, and Wachsmann's books, *The Sea of Galilee Boat: An Extraordinary 2000-Year-Old Discovery* (New York: Plenum Press, 1995), and *The Excavations of an Ancient Boat in the Sea of Galilee (Lake Kinneret),* Atiquot 19 (Jerusalem: Israel Antiquities Authority, 1990).

Market Centers (pp. 140–144)

1. Information on coastal cities such as Tyre, Sidon, Dor, and others has been found in the following publications: Eric Meyers, "Galilee in the Time of Jesus," *Archaeology* 47, no. 6 (November–December 1994): 41; J. D. Douglas, ed., *Illustrated Bible Dictionary,* vol. 1 (Sydney and Auckland: Intervarsity Press, 1980); *Dictionnaire de la Bible* (Paris: Librairie Letouzey and Ané, 1922), 5:1, 7; Avner Raban and Robert Stieglitz, "The Sea Peoples and Their Contributions to Civilization," *Biblical Archaeology Review* 17, no. 6 (November–December 1991): 34–42; Samuel Mathews, "The Phoenicians: Sea Lords of Antiquity," *National Geographic* 146, no. 2 (August 1974): 149–89. I am also familiar with the story that Jesus' putative father, a Roman soldier named Pantera, came from Sidon, which some have held to be a plausible reason for his visit. See John J. Rousseau and Rami Arav, eds., *Jesus and His World: An Archaeological and Cultural Dictionary* (Minneapolis: Fortress Press, 1995), 223–25; 326–28. There is also apparently a tradition among Maronite villages in northern Galilee that as a young man Jesus embarked on a Tyrian vessel as a shipwright and voyaged to the

west coast of Britain and spent the winter there. There are numerous British legends about the young Jesus spending time there, so that contact with the coastal cities as embarkation points for such a journey would be necessary. See Rt. Rev. Robert C. Harvey, *To the Isles Afar Off: Traditions of the Early British Church* (Victoria, Tex.: Foundation for Christian Theology, 1980), 3.

2. Willard Bascom, *Deep Water, Ancient Ships* (Garden City, N.Y.: Doubleday, 1976), and Douglas Edwards, "The Socio-Economic and Cultural Ethos of the Lower Galilee of the First Century: Implications for the Nascent Jesus Movement," in *The Galilee in Late Antiquity,* ed. Lee Levine (New York: Jewish Theological Seminary of North America, 1992), 55, both contain discussions of trading patterns and networks in Galilee and the Roman Empire of Jesus' time.

3. *Interpreter's Dictionary of the Bible* (New York: Abingdon, 1962), 4:337.

Competition and Cooperation (pp. 148–152)

1. See, for example, Raoul Andersen regarding secrecy and protection of knowledge of where to fish and when: "Hunt and Deceive: Information Management in Newfoundland Deep Sea Trawler Fishing," in *North Atlantic Fishermen: Anthropological Essays on Modern Fishing,* ed. Raoul Andersen and Cato Wadel, Newfoundland Social and Economic Papers, no. 5 (St. John's, Newfoundland: Memorial University of Newfoundland, 1972), 120–40. The literature of maritime anthropology contains numerous examples of studies regarding fishermen's communication techniques.

2. W. H. Wuellner, *The Meaning of "Fishers of Men"* (Philadelphia: Westminster Press, 1967), 9.

3. Chapter 10, verses 1–7, "Gospel of Mary," in *The Complete Gospels,* ed. Robert Miller (Sonoma, Calif.: Polebridge Press, 1992), 359.

The Fishermen's Pentecost (pp. 153–160)

1. Shelley Wachsmann, *The Sea of Galilee Boat: An Extraordinary 2000-Year-Old Discovery* (New York: Plenum Press, 1995), 326–28.

2. Raymond Moody, *Life after Life* (New York: Bantam, 1977), 170–73.

3. *The New American Bible for Catholics* (Iowa Falls, Iowa: World Bible Publishers, 1991), 1021.

4. Dean Badger, personal communication.

Language as Code (pp. 161–164)

1. Albert Nolan, *Jesus before Christianity* (Maryknoll, N.Y.: Orbis Books, 2001), 62, 177, and Joachim Jeremias, *The Parables of Jesus,* 2d rev. ed. (New York: Scribner, 1972), 195.

Spotting God (pp. 165–168)

1. Interview with Gunnar Hermanson by Lawrence Johnson, November 7, 1988, Astoria, Oregon, Columbia River Maritime Museum, 25.

2. Eric Maple, "Fish," in *Man, Myth, and Magic: The Illustrated Encyclopedia of Mythology, Religion, and the Unknown,* ed. Richard Cavendish (New York: Marshall Cavendish, 1985), 4:984.

The End of Time in Shades of Silver (pp. 175–180)

1. Interview with Bill Gunderson by Jim Bergeron, December 16, 1988. Astoria, Oregon, Columbia River Maritime Museum, 8.

2. Poem courtesy Hobe Kytr.

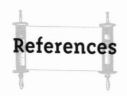

References

Unpublished

Columbia River Gillnetters Oral History Project. A joint project of Oregon Sea Grant and the Columbia River Maritime Museum. Interviews housed at Columbia River Maritime Museum, Astoria, Oregon.

Reed, Jonathan. "Places in Early Christianity: Galilee, Archaeology, Urbanization, and Q." Ph.D. Diss., Claremont Graduate School. Ann Arbor, Mich.: University Microfilms International, 1994.

Books

Abrahamsen, Valerie. *Women and Worship at Philippi: Diana/Artemis and Other Cults in the Early Christian Era.* Portland, Me.: Astarte Shell Press, 1995.

Achtemeier, Paul, ed. *Harper's Bible Dictionary.* San Francisco: HarperSanFrancisco, 1985.

Aland, Kurt, et al. *The Greek New Testament.* New York: American Bible Society, 1975.

Allison, Charlene, Sue-Ellen Jacobs, and Mary Porter. *Winds of Change: Women in Northwest Commercial Fishing.* Seattle: University of Washington Press, 1989.

Alter, Robert, and Frank Kermode. *The Literary Guide to the Bible.* Cambridge, Mass.: Belknap Press of Harvard University Press, 1987.

Andersen, Raoul, ed. *North Atlantic Maritime Cultures.* The Hague: Mouton, 1979.

Andersen, Raoul, and Cato Wadel, eds. *North Atlantic Fishermen, Anthropological Essays on Modern Fishing.* St. John's, Newfoundland.: Memorial University of Newfoundland, 1972. Newfoundland Social and Economic Papers, No. 5.

Arav, Rami, and Richard Freund, eds. *Bethsaida: A City by the North Shore of the Sea of Galilee.* 2 vols. Kirksville, Mo.: Thomas Jefferson University Press, 1995; Truman State University Press, 1999.

Barclay, William. *The Master's Men.* New York: Abingdon, 1959.

Barker, William. *Everyone in the Bible.* Tappan, N.J.: Fleming Revell, 1966.

Barnstone, Willis, ed. *The Other Bible.* San Francisco: HarperSanFrancisco, 1984.

Bascom, Willard. *Deep Water, Ancient Ships.* Garden City, N.Y.: Doubleday, 1976.

Bittleman, Sarah. *Commercial Fishers: An Endangered Species.* New York: Seamen's Church Institute of New York and New Jersey, 1980.

Borg, Marcus. *Jesus, A New Vision: Spirit, Culture and the Life of Discipleship.* San Francisco: HarperSanFrancisco, 1987.

Borg, Marcus, and N. T. Wright. *The Meaning of Jesus: Two Visions.* San Francisco: HarperSanFrancisco, 1999.

Buttrick, George, ed. *The Interpreter's Bible.* Vol. 7. New York: Abingdon, 1951.

———. *Interpreter's Dictionary of the Bible.* Vols. 2, 3, 4. New York: Abingdon, 1962.

Casson, Lionel. *The Ancient Mariners.* Princeton, N.J.: Princeton University Press, 1991.

———. *Ships and Seamanship in the Ancient World.* 2d ed. Princeton, N.J.: Princeton University Press, 1986.

Catholic Bishops of the [Northwest] Region. *The Columbia River Watershed: Caring for Creation and the Common Good.* An International Pastoral Letter by the Catholic Bishops of the Region. January 8, 2001.

Cavendish, Richard, ed. *Man, Myth, and Magic: The Illustrated Encyclopedia of Mythology, Religion, and the Unknown.* Vol. 4. New York: Marshall Cavendish, 1985.

Child, Heather, and Dorothy Colles. *Christian Symbols, Ancient and Modern: A Handbook for Students.* London, G. Bell and Sons, 1971.

Cordell, John, ed. *A Sea of Small Boats.* Cultural Survival Report 26. Cambridge, Mass.: Cultural Survival, Inc., 1989.

Cross, F. L., and E. A. Livingstone, eds. *The Oxford Dictionary of the Christian Church.* 2d ed. London: Oxford University Press, 1974.

Crossan, John Dominic. *The Birth of Christianity.* San Francisco: HarperSanFrancisco, 1998.

———. *The Historical Jesus: The Life of a Mediterranean Jewish Peasant.* San Francisco: HarperSanFrancisco, 1992.

———. *Jesus: A Revolutionary Biography.* San Francisco: HarperSanFrancisco, 1994.

Crossan, John Dominic, and Jonathan Reed. *Excavating Jesus: Beneath the Stones, Behind the Texts.* San Francisco: HarperSanFrancisco, 2001.

Danowski, Fran. *Fishermen's Wives: Coping with an Extraordinary Occupation.* Marine Bulletin 37. Narragansett: University of Rhode Island, 1980.

Davis, John. *Davis Dictionary of the Bible.* Grand Rapids, Mich.: Baker Book House, 1983.

Dean, Edith. *All of the Women of the Bible.* New York: Harper, 1955.

De la Varende, Jean. *Cherish the Sea: A History of Sail.* New York: Viking, 1956.

Douglas, J. D., ed. *Illustrated Bible Dictionary.* Vol. 1. Sydney and Auckland: Intervarsity Press, 1980.

Drane, John. *Introducing the New Testament.* San Francisco: Harper and Row, 1986.

Dyer, Christopher, and James McGoodwin, eds. *Folk Management in the World's Fisheries.* Niwot: University Press of Colorado, 1994.

Edey, Maitland, and the Editors. *The Sea Traders.* Alexandria, Va.: Time-Life Books, 1974.

Eisen, Ute. *Women Officeholders in Early Christianity.* Collegeville, Minn.: Liturgical Press, 2000.

Encyclopaedia Judaica. Vol. 6. Jerusalem: Macmillan, 1971.

Encyclopedia of World Art. Vol. 11. New York: McGraw Hill, 1966.

Fields, Leslie Leyland. *The Entangling Net: Alaska's Commercial Fishing Women Tell Their Lives.* Urbana: University of Illinois Press, 1997.

Finegan, Jack. *The Archeology of the New Testament.* Princeton, N.J.: Princeton University Press, 1992.

Flinder, Alexander. *Secrets of the Bible Seas.* London: Severn House Publishers, 1985.

Foster, George. *Peasant Society: A Reader.* Boston: Little, Brown, 1967.

Frazer, Sir James. *The Illustrated Golden Bough.* New York: Simon and Schuster, 1996.

Fredriksen, Paula. *From Jesus to Christ: The Origins of the New Testament Images of Jesus.* New Haven: Yale University Press, 1988.

Frye, Northrop. *The Great Code.* Toronto: Academic Press Canada, 1982.

Funk, Robert. *Honest to Jesus.* San Francisco: HarperSanFrancisco (Polebridge Press), 1996.

Funk, Robert, Roy Hoover, and the Jesus Seminar. *The Five Gospels: The Search for the Authentic Words of Jesus.* New York: Macmillan (Polebridge Press), 1993.

Garrity-Blake, Barbara J. *To Fish or Not to Fish: Occupational Transitions within the Commercial Fishing Community of Carteret County, N.C.* North Carolina Sea Grant Technical Report 96–05. Greenville, N.C.: East Carolina University Press, 1996.

Gilden, Jennifer, and Courtland Smith. *Adapting to Change: Survey of Gillnetters in Oregon and Washington, Summary of Results.* Corvallis, Ore.: Oregon Sea Grant, 1996.

Gillquist, Fr. Peter, Project Director. *The Orthodox Study Bible.* Nashville: Thomas Nelson, 1993.

Goodenough, Edwin. *Jewish Symbols in the Greco-Roman Period: Fish, Bread, and Wine.* Bollingen Series 37. Vols. 5, 6. New York: Pantheon Books, 1956.

Goodman, Martin. *State and Society in Roman Galilee.* Totowa, N.J.: Rowman and Allanheld, 1983.

Goodspeed, Edgar. *The Twelve.* Philadelphia: John C. Winston, 1957.

Grollenberg, Luc. *The Penguin Shorter Atlas of the Bible.* New York: Penguin, 1959.

Harley, Basil. *Church Ships: A Handbook of Votive and Commemorative Models.* Norwich: Canterbury Press, 1994.

Harvey, Rt. Rev. Robert C. *To the Isles Afar Off: Traditions of the Early British Church.* Victoria, Tex.: Foundation for Christian Theology, 1980.

Haskins, Susan. *Mary Magdalen: Myth and Metaphor.* New York: Harcourt, Brace, 1993.

Hastings, James. *Dictionary of the Bible.* 5 vols. New York: Charles Scribner's Sons, 1898–1904.

———. *Dictionary of the Bible.* Rev. ed. New York: Charles Scribner's Sons, 1963.

Haws, Duncan. *Ships and the Sea.* London: Hart, Davis and Mac-Gibbon, 1976.

Hennecke, Edgar. *New Testament Apocrypha.* Vol. 1. Philadelphia: Westminster, 1963.

Hoskins, Sir Edwyn. *The Fourth Gospel.* London: Faber and Faber, 1947.

Jeremias, Joachim. *The Parables of Jesus.* 2d rev. ed. New York: Scribner, 1972.

Jöckle, Clemens. *Encyclopedia of Saints.* London: Alpine, 1995.

Josephus, Flavius. *The Works of Josephus.* Translated by William Whiston. Peabody, Mass.: Hendrickson, 1987.

Jung, Carl G. *Aion: Researches into the Phenomenology of the Self.* Bollingen Series 20. Princeton: Princeton University Press, 1978.

Keller, Phillip. *A Shepherd Looks at Psalm 23.* New York: Harper, 1970.

Kemp, Peter, ed. *The Oxford Companion to Ships and the Sea.* London: Oxford University Press, 1976.

Kraeling, Emil. *Rand McNally Bible Atlas.* New York: Rand McNally, 1956.

Levine, Lee, ed. *The Galilee in Late Antiquity.* New York: Jewish Theological Seminary of America, 1992.

Loffreda, Stanislao. *Recovering Capharnaum.* 2d ed. Jerusalem: Franciscan Printing Press, 1993.

McBirnie, William S. *The Search for the Twelve Apostles.* Wheaton, Ill.: Tyndale House, 1973.

MacGregor, John. *The Rob Roy on the Jordan, Nile, Red Sea, & Gennesareth, &c.: A Canoe Cruise in Palestine and Egypt, and the Waters of Damascus.* London: John Murray, 1869, reprint by Long Riders' Guild Press, 2001.

McKenzie, John. *Dictionary of the Bible.* New York: Macmillan, 1965.

McManners, John, ed. *The Oxford Illustrated History of Christianity.* Oxford: Oxford University Press, 1990.

Malina, Bruce. *The New Testament World, Insights from Cultural Anthropology.* Atlanta: John Knox, 1981.

Marshall, Alfred, trans. *The R.S.V. Interlinear Greek-English New Testament.* Grand Rapids, Mich.: Zondervan, 1978.

Martin, Irene. *Legacy and Testament: The Story of Columbia River Gillnetters.* Pullman, Wash.: Washington State University Press, 1994.

Maus, Cynthia. *Christ and the Fine Arts.* New York: Harper, 1938.

May, Herbert, and Bruce Metzger. *The New Oxford Annotated Bible with the Apocrypha, Revised Standard Version.* New York: Oxford University Press, 1977.

Mays, James, ed. *Harper's Bible Commentary.* San Francisco: HarperSanFrancisco, 1988.

Meeks, Wayne, ed. *The HarperCollins Study Bible.* New York: HarperCollins, 1993.

Metzger, Bruce, and Michael Coogan. *The Oxford Companion to the Bible.* New York: Oxford University Press, 1993.

Millar, Fergus. *The Roman Near East, 31 B.C.–A.D. 337.* Cambridge, Mass.: Harvard University Press, 1993.

Miller, Robert, ed. *The Complete Gospels.* Sonoma, Calif.: Polebridge Press, 1992.

Moody, Raymond. *Life after Life.* New York: Bantam, 1977.

New American Bible for Catholics. Iowa Falls, Iowa: World Bible Publishers, 1991.

Neyrey, Jerome, ed. *The Social World of Luke-Acts: Models for Interpretation.* Peabody, Mass.: Hendrickson, 1991.

Nolan, Albert. *Jesus before Christianity.* Maryknoll, N.Y.: Orbis Books, 2001.

Nun, Mendel. *The Sea of Galilee and Its Fishermen in the New Testament.* Kibbutz Ein Gev, Israel: Tourist Department and Kinnereth Sailing Co., 1989.

O'Driscoll, Herbert. *For All the Saints.* Cambridge, Mass.: Cowley, 1995.

Oesterly, W. *A History of Israel.* Vol. 2. Oxford: Clarendon Press, 1951.

Orchard, Bernard, et al., eds. *Catholic Commentary on Holy Scripture*. London: Thomas Nelson, 1953.

Panayotou, Theodore. *Territorial Use Rights in Fisheries*. FAO Fish Report No. 289, Supplement. Rome: United Nations Food and Agricultural Organization, 1984.

Phillips, J. B. *Peter's Portrait of Jesus*. Cleveland: Collins, World, 1976.

Platt, Rutherford, ed. *The Lost Books of the Bible and the Forgotten Books of Eden*. Cleveland: World Publishing, 1963.

Price, Reynolds. *Three Gospels*. New York: Scribner, 1996.

Pyle, Robert Michael. *The Thunder Tree: Lessons from an Urban Wildland*. Boston: Houghton Mifflin, 1993.

Reader's Digest. *Atlas of the Bible*. Pleasantville, N.Y.: Reader's Digest Association, 1981.

Reader's Digest. *The Last Two Million Years*. London: Reader's Digest Association, 1974.

Rihbany, Abraham. *The Syrian Christ*. Boston: Houghton Mifflin, 1916.

Roberts, Rev. Alexander, and James Donaldson, eds. *The Ante-Nicene Fathers*. Vol. 3. Grand Rapids, Mich.: Wm. B. Eerdmans, 1986.

Robinson, John. *The Priority of John*. Minneapolis: Fortress Press, 1985.

Rogerson, John. *The Cultural Atlas of the World: The Bible*. Alexandria, Va.: Stonehenge Press, 1992.

Rostovtzeff, M. *The Social and Economic History of the Hellenistic World*. Vol. 1. Oxford: Clarendon Press, 1953.

———. *The Social and Economic History of the Roman Empire*. 2d ed. Vol. 3. Oxford: Clarendon Press, 1957.

Rousmaniere, Leah. *Anchored within the Vail: A Pictorial History of the Seamen's Church Institute*. New York: Seamen's Church Institute of New York and New Jersey, 1995.

Rousseau, John, and Rami Arav. *Jesus and His World: An Archaeological and Cultural Dictionary*. Minneapolis: Fortress Press, 1995.

Russell, D. S. *The Jews from Alexander to Herod*. London: Oxford University Press, 1967.

St. John, Robert. *Roll Jordan Roll.* Garden City, N.Y.: Doubleday, 1965.

Sasson, Jack, ed. *Civilizations of the Ancient Near East.* Vol. 1. New York: Simon and Schuster and Prentice Hall International, 1995.

Shanks, Hershel, ed. *The Search for Jesus: Modern Scholarship Looks at the Gospels.* Symposium at the Smithsonian Institution, September 11, 1993. Washington, D.C.: Biblical Archaeology Society, 1994.

Smith, George Adam. *The Historical Geography of the Holy Land.* London: Hodder and Stoughton, 1897.

Spong, John Shelby. *Resurrection: Myth or Reality?* San Francisco: HarperSanFrancisco, 1994.

Stern, Ephraim. *New Encyclopedia of Archaeological Excavations in the Holy Land.* 4 vols. New York: Simon and Schuster, 1993.

Telushkin, Joseph. *Jewish Literacy.* New York: William Morrow, 1991.

Tzaferis, Vassilios. *Excavations at Capernaum, 1978–1982.* Winona Lake, Ind.: Eisenbrauns, 1989.

———. *The Excavations of Kursi-Gergesa.* Atiquot 16, English Series. Jerusalem: Department of Antiquities and Museums, 1983.

Van Beck, Todd. *The Cemetery History Book.* Covington, Ky.: Loewen Group, 1994.

Vigouroux, F., ed. *Dictionnaire de la Bible.* Paris: Librairie Letouzey and Ané, 1922.

Wachsmann, Shelley. *The Excavations of an Ancient Boat in the Sea of Galilee (Lake Kinneret).* Atiquot 19. Jerusalem: Israel Antiquities Authority, 1990.

Wachsmann, Shelley. *The Sea of Galilee Boat: An Extraordinary 2000-Year-Old Discovery.* New York: Plenum Press, 1995.

Walker, Alexander. *An Account of a Voyage to the Northwest Coast of America in 1785 and 1786.* Ed. Robin Fisher and J. Bumsted. Seattle: University of Washington Press, 1982.

Weatherhead, Leslie. *It Happened in Palestine.* New York: Abingdon Press, 1936.

Wiles, Maurice, ed. *Documents in Early Christian Thought.* Cambridge: Cambridge University Press, 1975.

Wilson, A. N. *Jesus.* New York: W. W. Norton, 1992.

World Book, Inc. *World Book Encyclopedia.* Vol. 6. Chicago: World Book, 1994.

Wuellner, W. H. *The Meaning of "Fishers of Men."* Philadelphia: Westminster, 1967.

Articles

Ainsworth, Percy. "The Miraculous Draught of Fishes." *Weavings* 16, no. 2 (March–April 2001): 24–30.

Andersen, Raoul. "Hunt and Deceive: Information Management in Newfoundland Deep-sea Trawler Fishing." In *North Atlantic Fishermen: Anthropological Essays on Modern Fishing,* ed. Raoul Andersen and Cato Wadel. Newfoundland Social and Economic Papers No. 5. St. John's, Newfoundland: Memorial University of Newfoundland, 1972.

Anderson, Eugene. "Fish as Gods and Kin." In *Folk Management in the World's Fisheries,* ed. Christopher Dyer and James McGoodwin, 139–60. Niwot: University Press of Colorado, 1994.

Arav, Rami, Richard Freund, and John Shroder Jr. "Bethsaida Rediscovered." *Biblical Archaeology Review* 26, no. 1 (January–February 2000): 44–56.

Arden, Harvey. "The Living Dead Sea." *National Geographic* 153, no. 2 (February 1978): 224–45.

Bates, Richard. "Sepphoris: An Urban Portrait of Jesus." *Biblical Archaeology Review* 18, no. 3 (May–June 1992): 50–62.

Belt, Don. "Living in the Shadow of Peace — Israel's Galilee." *National Geographic* 187, no. 6 (June 1995): 62–87.

Bishop, Eric. "Jesus and the Lake." *Catholic Biblical Quarterly* 13 (1951): 398–414.

Borg, Marcus. "The Palestinian Background for a Life of Jesus." In *The Search for Jesus: Modern Scholarship Looks at the Gospels.* Symposium at the Smithsonian Institution, September 11, 1993. Washington, D.C.: Biblical Archaeology Society, 1994.

Boyer, David. "Geographical Twins a World Apart." *National Geographic* 114, no. 6 (December 1958): 848–59.

Burrell, Barbara, Kathryn Gleason, and Ehud Netzer. "Uncovering Herod's Seaside Palace." *Biblical Archaeology Review* 19, no. 3 (May–June 1993): 50–57, 76.

211

Butzer, Karl. "Environmental Change in the Near East and Human Impact on the Land." In *Civilizations of the Ancient Near East,* ed. Jack Sasson, 1:123–51. New York: Simon and Schuster and Prentice Hall International, 1995.

Chancey, Mark, and Eric Meyers. "How Jewish Was Sepphoris in Jesus' Time?" *Biblical Archaeology Review* 26, no. 4 (July–August 2000): 18–33, 61.

Chattaway, Peter. "Jesus in the Movies." *Bible Review* 14, no. 1 (February 1998): 28–35, 45–46.

Cleave, Richard. "Satellite Revelations: New Views of the Holy Land." *National Geographic* 187, no. 6 (June 1995): 88–105.

Coogan, Michael. "Canaanites: Who Were They and Where Did They Live?" *Bible Review* 9, no. 3 (June 1993) 44–45.

Cooksey, Chris. "Bibliography of Tyrian Purple." Originally published in *Dyes in History and Archaeology* 12 (1994): 57–66. Updated at *www.chriscooksey.demon.co.uk/tyrian/cjcbiblio.html.*

Creed, Carolyn. "It's Not a Job, It's a Lifestyle." *Cross Currents* 2 (Autumn 1988): 85–92.

Doney, Carl. "Fisherman or Shepherd." In *The Pacific Northwest Pulpit,* comp. Paul Little, 45–57. New York: Methodist Book Concern, 1915.

Doubilet, David. "The Desert Sea." *National Geographic* 184, no. 5 (November 1993): 60–87.

Dutcher-Walls, Patricia. "Sociological Directions in Feminist Biblical Studies." *Social Compass* 46, no. 4 (1999): 441–53.

Edwards, Douglas. "The Socio-Economic and Cultural Ethos of the Lower Galilee in the First Century: Implications for the Nascent Jesus Movement." In *The Galilee in Late Antiquity,* ed. Lee Levine. New York: Jewish Theological Seminary of North America, 1992.

Emerton, J. A. "The Hundred and Fifty-Three Fishes in John 21:11." *Journal of Theological Studies* (April 1958): 86–89.

"Fishermen Face New Era on the Sea of Galilee." *The Fish Boat* (April 1987): 29.

Fleming, Carol. "Maidens of the Sea can be Alluring, but Sailor, Beware." *Smithsonian* 14, no. 3 (June 1983) 86–95.

Flemming, N. C., A. Raban, and C. Goetschel. "Tectonic and Eu-
static Changes on the Mediterranean Coast of Israel in the Last
9000 Years." In *Beneath the Waters of Time: The Proceedings of
the Ninth Conference on Underwater Archaeology,* ed. J. Barto
Arnold III, 129–57. Publication No. 6. Austin: Texas Antiquities
Committee, 1978.

"The Greenland Whale Fishery." *Sea Heritage News* 13 (1983): 28.

Hanson, K. C. "The Galilean Fishing Economy and the Jesus
Tradition." *Biblical Theology Bulletin* 27, no. 3 (Fall 1997):
99–111.

Heidorn, Keith. "Weather Phenomenon and Elements: The Fire of
St. Elmo." *The Weather Doctor, Spectrum Educational Enterprises,* May 30, 1998. Website *www.islandnet.com.*

Hohlfelder, Robert. "Herod the Great's City on the Sea: Caesarea
Maritima." *National Geographic* 171, no. 2 (February 1987):
260–79.

Kee, Howard C. "Sociology of the New Testament." In *Harper's
Bible Dictionary,* ed. Paul Achtemeier, 961–73. San Francisco:
HarperSanFrancisco, 1985.

Kinch, John. "Love of Life." *Nature Conservancy* 46, no. 2 (March–
April 1996): 8–9.

La Fay, Howard. "Where Jesus Walked." *National Geographic* 132,
no. 6 (December 1967): 739–81.

Leach, Edmund. "Fishing for Men on the Edge of the Wilderness." In
The Literary Guide to the Bible, ed. Robert Alter and Frank Ker-
mode, 579–99. Cambridge, Mass.: Belknap Press of Harvard
University Press, 1987.

Linder, Elisha. "Excavating an Ancient Merchantman." *Biblical
Archaeology Review* 18, no. 6 (November–December 1992):
24–35.

McCay, Bonnie. "Systems Ecology, People Ecology and the Anthropology of Fishing Communities." *Human Ecology* 6, no. 4
(1978): 397–422.

MacLeish, Kenneth. "The Land of Galilee." *National Geographic* 128,
no. 6 (December 1965): 832–65.

Maple, Eric. "Fish." In *Man, Myth and Magic: The Illustrated Encyclopedia of Mythology, Religion, and the Unknown,* ed. Richard
Cavendish, 4:983–87. New York: Marshall Cavendish, 1985.

Margulis, Lynn. "Talking on the Water." *Sierra* 79, no. 3 (May–June 1994): 72–75.

Martin, Irene. "Jesus and the Fishermen of the Bible." *National Fisherman Yearbook* (1982).

Martin, Kent. "Play by the Rules or Don't Play at All: Space Division and Resource Allocation in a Rural Newfoundland Fishing Community." In *North Atlantic Maritime Cultures,* ed. Raoul Andersen, 277–98. The Hague: Mouton, 1979.

Matthews, Samuel. "The Phoenicians: Sea Lords of Antiquity." *National Geographic* 146, no. 2 (August 1974): 149–89.

Meyers, Eric. "Galilee in the Time of Jesus." *Archaeology* 47, no. 6 (November–December 1994): 41.

Moses, Paul. "The New Face of Jesus." *Daily News* (Longview, Wash.), April 7, 2001, C1, C4.

Nun, Mendel. "Cast Your Net upon the Water: Fish and Fishermen in Jesus' Time." *Biblical Archaeology Review* 19, no. 6 (November–December 1993): 46–56, 70.

Nun, Mendel. "Ports of Galilee." *Biblical Archaeology Review* 25, no. 4 (July–August 1999): 19–31, 64.

Oakman, Douglas. "Was Jesus a Peasant? Implications for Reading the Samaritan Story." *Biblical Theology Bulletin* 22 (1992): 117–25.

Olson, Donna. "Georgia Maki, Astoria Net Mender." In *North Coast Folklife Festival,* ed. Suzi Jones, 19–21. Astoria, Ore.: Oregon Arts Commission, 1977.

Oren, O. H. "Physical and Chemical Characteristics of Lake Tiberias." *Bulletin of the Research Council of Israel* 11G, no. 1 (May 1962): 1–33.

Palmer, Sean. "St. Elmo's Fire." *Earth Light Resource, 1999–2002.* Website *www.mysterylights.com.*

Patterson, Nancy Lou. *Women in the Church.* National Guild of Churchmen Tract, no. 121. Palm Desert, Calif.: National Guild of Churchmen, 1987.

"Phantom Ship Recorded on Film for the First Time." *Northern Light,* website at *http://collections.ic.gc.ca/vaisseaufantome/presse/presse11.html,* January 14, 1981.

Pollack, Susan. "City by the Sea." *Orion* 20, no. 1 (Winter 2001): 38–47.

P'til Tehkelet. "Top Ten Tekhelet FAQ's and Facts." Website for the Association for the Promotion and Distribution of Tekhelet, *www.tekhelet.com,* Jerusalem, 2001.

Raban, Avner, and Robert Stieglitz. "The Sea Peoples and Their Contributions to Civilization." *Biblical Archaeology Review* 17, no. 6 (November–December 1991): 34–42.

Robbins, Vernon K. "The Social Location of the Implied Author." In *The Social World of Luke/Acts,* ed. Jerome Neyrey, 305–32. Peabody, Mass.: Hendrickson, 1991.

Rynor, Michah. "Market Power." *University of Toronto Magazine* (Summer 1999): 7.

Sheler, Jeffery. "Days of the Martyrs." *U.S. News and World Report,* April 16, 2001, 41–45.

Shenhav, Dodo. "Loaves and Fishes Mosaic near Sea of Galilee Restored." *Biblical Archaeology Review* 10, no. 3 (May–June 1984): 22–31.

Shimoda, Jerry. "Pu'uhonua-Honaunau: Place of Refuge." *National Parks and Conservation Magazine/The Environmental Journal* (February 1975): 4–9.

Silberman, Neil. "Searching for Jesus: The Politics of First Century Judea." *Archaeology* 47, no. 6 (November–December 1994): 30–41.

Simpson, Pat. "Church of Mary Magdalene." *Annual Source Newsletter.* Church Council of Greater Seattle (November 1998): 1, 2.

Smith, Courtland. "Connecting Cultural and Biological Diversity in Restoring Northwest Salmon." *Fisheries* 19, no. 2 (February 1994): 20–26.

Smith, Courtland, and Susan Hanna. "Occupation and Community as Determinants of Fishing Behaviors." *Human Organization* 52, no. 3 (Fall 1993): 299–303.

Smith, M. Estellie. "Comments on the Heuristic Utility of Maritime Anthropology." *Maritime Anthropologist* 1, no. 1 (Summer 1977): 2–8.

Stern, Ephraim. "The Persistence of Phoenician Culture." *Biblical Archaeology Review* 19, no. 3 (May–June 1993): 38–49.

Stickan, Walter. "Bioluminescence and Diurnal Rhythmicity in Dinoflagellates." Website at *www.iwf.de/iwfeng/3medien/33db/333/c2013.html.*

Stieglitz, Robert. "Hydraulic and Fishing Installations at Tel Tanninim." *Near Eastern Archaeology* 61, no. 4 (1998): 256.

Sudilovsky, Judith. "A Lot More Than Oranges: Egyptian Finds Uncovered in Jaffa." *Biblical Archaeology Review* 26, no. 2 (March–April 2000): 18.

Toperoff, S. P. "Fish in Bible and Midrash." *Dor Le Dor* 16, no. 1 (1987): 46–50.

Tzaferis, Vassilios. "A Pilgrimage to the Site of the Swine Miracle." *Biblical Archaeology Review* 14, no. 2 (March–April 1989): 45–51.

Wachsmann, Shelley. "The Galilee Boat: 2000-Year-Old Hull Recovered Intact." *Biblical Archaeology Review* 14, no. 5 (September–October 1988): 18–33.

Wakefield, Dan. "Clear Vision [Interview with Reynolds Price]." *Common Boundary* 14, no. 4 (July–August 1996): 22–29.

Zias, Joseph. "Anthropological Observations." Page 25 in *The Excavations of an Ancient Boat in the Sea of Galilee (Lake Kinneret)*, ed. Shelley Wachsmann, 125 Atiquot 19. Jerusalem: Israel Antiquities Authority, 1990.

Media

Work Is Our Joy: The Story of the Columbia River Gillnetter. Video. Written by Irene Martin. Produced by Lawrence Johnson. Oregon State University Extension Sea Grant and Columbia River Maritime Museum, 1989.

Acknowledgments

The following people have helped in some way to fashion this book: Elise Astleford, Larry McCagg, Blaine Hammond, Ed Wilson, Palmer Partington, Rick Bayles, Ed Rankin, Richard and Ann Hicks, Bob Rhodes, Robin Moore, the members of the Columbia Region Clericus, the congregation at St. James Episcopal Church, Cathlamet, Steve Petraitis, Dean and Gerry Badger, Sig Bakke, Jack and Georgia Marincovich, Jim Bergeron, Bob Eaton, Bobbi McAllister, Jack and Elaine Edwards, the fishermen of the Columbia and other areas, including Newfoundland, Hawaii, Great Britain, and the west coast of North America. Writer friends include John Freeman, Thomas Vaughan and Elizabeth Crownhart Vaughan, Rick Minor, Kathryn Toepel, Ruth Kirk, Hobe Kytr, Keith Petersen, Jim Lemonds, Cathy Zimmerman, Joan Lemieux, Rick Seifert, Jane Elder Wulff, and Bob and Thea Pyle. Thanks to Bill Wagner for his photo work.

Patient librarians include Jan Matsumoto and Tovi Harris at Diocese of Olympia Resource Center, those at the Longview Public Library, Skamokawa Community Library, Cathlamet City Library, and public libraries in Wrangell and Petersburg, the Washington State Library, Multnomah County Library, Oregon Historical Society Library, the Royal Ontario Museum, the University of Toronto and Toronto Public Library, and Memorial University of Newfoundland libraries. The Columbia River Maritime Museum collection was extremely useful. Special thanks to Dave Pearson, Curator, and Jerry Ostermiller, Director. The *Biblical Archaeology Review* helped locate a couple of hard-to-find publications. The Washington Dept. of Fish and Wildlife and Oregon Dept. of Fisheries and Wildlife, particularly the Columbia River biologists, have provided occasional source material.

Other friends include the Blix family, Ruth Sandvik, David Nelson, Steve and Debbie McClain, Carol Carver, George Exum, Rachael Wolford, John Wolford, Bruce and Diantha Weilepp, J'Anne Hook, Duncan Cruickshank, Heidi Heywood, Ruby Murray, David Vik, and many others to whom I extend my gratitude for their kindness and support. Family members include my mother- and father-in-law, my brother- and sister-in-law, my parents, who believed I could write, my husband, Kent, my daughters, Varsha and Menoka, and my granddaughter, Ariele (Dagmar).

I would especially like to thank Roy M. Carlisle, Senior Editor, of Crossroad Carlisle Books and the entire team at The Crossroad Publishing Company, for their patience, good humor, and enthusiasm.

Finally, I believe that this book has been a gift from God, who gave the insights, the ideas and the time to live it and then write it down.

About the Author

Born in England, raised in Canada, and a thirty-year resident of the United States, Irene Martin has spent over half her life among maritime cultures. She has fished with her husband, Kent, in Alaska and on the Columbia River and Willapa Bay. Active in environmental issues associated with the Columbia River, she has been an advisor to the Columbia River Estuary Data Development Program, a board member of Salmon For All, and is currently a board member on the Lower Columbia Regional Fisheries Enhancement Group.

She has used this fishing background in articles and books in her writing career. Previous works include *Legacy and Testament: The Story of Columbia River Gillnetters* and *The Beach of Heaven: A History of Wahkiakum County,* both published by Washington State University Press. These works garnered her the James Castles Heritage Award (1998) and the Governor's Heritage Award (2000). She wrote the script for the video production *Work Is Our Joy,* the Story of the Columbia River Gillnetters, winner of the Golden Reel Award from the National Federation of Community Broadcasters, 1990. She is also the author of *Lewis and Clark in the Land of the Wahkiakums* (Scrub Jay Press, 2003).

Irene Martin is an Episcopal priest serving St. James Episcopal Church in Cathlamet, Washington. *Sea Fire* incorporates her knowledge of and appreciation for fishing and fishing cultures with an analysis of the Bible that is unique in religious literature. She says, "I spent many hours on board the *Blue Mist* just looking at the beauty around me and letting it speak to me. I wanted to express Jesus' involvement in the fishing life of the Sea of Galilee in a way that integrates scholarship and my own experience." *Sea Fire* is the result of years of patient observation, thoughtful reflection on scripture, and modern scholarship, and fishing adventures on the Northwest coast.

Scripture Index

Subject Index